Python Projects for Kids

Unleash Python and take your small readers on an adventurous ride through the world of programming

Jessica Ingrassellino

BIRMINGHAM - MUMBAI

Python Projects for Kids

First published: April 2016

Production reference: 1070416

Published by Packt Publishing Ltd.
Livery Place
35 Livery Street
Birmingham B3 2PB, UK.

ISBN 978-1-78217-506-3

www.packtpub.com

Credits

Author
Jessica Ingrassellino

Reviewer
David Whale

Commissioning Editor
Veena Pagare

Acquisition Editor
Aaron Lazar

Content Development Editor
Sachin Karnani

Technical Editor
Rupali R. Shrawane

Copy Editor
Sonia Cheema

Project Coordinator
Nikhil Nair

Proofreader
Safis Editing

Indexer
Rekha Nair

Production Coordinator
Melwyn Dsa

Cover Work
Melwyn Dsa

About the Author

Jessica Ingrassellino is a multi-talented educator, business leader, and technologist. She received her EdD from Teachers College, Columbia University for music education with an emphasis on assessment.

Jessica is currently employed as the lead software engineer in testing at Bitly, New York City. She transitioned from a teaching career of 10 years to a technology career through a balance of freelance work and social media exposure. Jessica's current work focuses on using Python to develop automated testing tools. She is an ASTQB certified quality assurance engineer with experience in testing web, mobile, and backend applications.

In addition to working at Bitly, Jessica remains committed to education and has founded `http://www.teachcode.org/`, a nonprofit that teaches computer programming skills to teachers and students in urban or underserved populations through Python and 2D game programming. This new initiative will give teachers the support they need through a standards-referenced curriculum, student-engaging activities, and access to experts in the field of technology.

I would like to thank my students for allowing me to have such fun teaching them Python and learning from their experiences as new programmers. I would also like to thank Cathy Kross and Alice McGowan for being willing to have me in their classes and school and interrupting their daily lives with my code-teaching experiments. Finally, I would like to thank my husband, Nick, for believing in me and helping me through some major writer's block. He never loses faith in me, and for that, I am eternally grateful.

About the Reviewer

David Whale is a software developer who lives in Essex, UK. He started coding as a schoolboy aged 11, inspired by his school's science technician to build his own computer from a kit. These early experiments lead to some of his code being used in a saleable educational word game when he was only 13.

David has been developing software professionally ever since, mainly writing embedded software that provides intelligence inside electronic products, including automated machinery, electric cars, mobile phones, energy meters, and wireless doorbells.

These days, David runs his own software consultancy called Thinking Binaries, and he spends about half of his time helping customers design software for new electronic products, many of which use Python. The rest of the time, he volunteers for The Institution of Engineering and Technology, running training courses for teachers, designing and running workshops and clubs for school children, running workshops and talks at meet-up events all round the UK, and generally being busy with his Raspberry Pi, BBC micro:bit, and Arduino.

David was the technical editor of *Adventures in Raspberry Pi, John Wiley & Sons*, the coauthor of *Adventures in Minecraft*, and he is a regular reviewer and editor of technical books for a number of book publishers.

I was really pleased to be asked to review this exciting new coding book for children. Python is an excellent language for children to learn from a young age, and Jessica has done a great job at helping readers take their first few steps in coding with Python. I hope you will be inspired by the code and ideas in this book and come up with your own ideas to enhance and develop all of the programs further—this is just the start of your exciting new creative journey into coding with Python!

www.PacktPub.com

eBooks, discount offers, and more

Did you know that Packt offers eBook versions of every book published, with PDF and ePub files available? You can upgrade to the eBook version at www.PacktPub.com and as a print book customer, you are entitled to a discount on the eBook copy. Get in touch with us at customercare@packtpub.com for more details.

At www.PacktPub.com, you can also read a collection of free technical articles, sign up for a range of free newsletters and receive exclusive discounts and offers on Packt books and eBooks.

https://www2.packtpub.com/books/subscription/packtlib

Do you need instant solutions to your IT questions? PacktLib is Packt's online digital book library. Here, you can search, access, and read Packt's entire library of books.

Why subscribe?

- Fully searchable across every book published by Packt
- Copy and paste, print, and bookmark content
- On demand and accessible via a web browser

Table of Contents

Preface

As you can guess from the title, this book is designed to teach the basic concepts of Python to kids. This book uses several mini projects so that kids can learn how to solve problems using Python.

Python has grown to become a very popular language for programming web apps, analyzing data, and teaching people how to write code. Python is known for being a simple language to use because it is read much like natural languages, yet it is able to do data analysis very quickly, making it a great language to create websites that handle a lot of data. Another nice thing about Python that makes it fun to use is that people have been working on game libraries, such as pygame, so that people can create graphics programs with Python. The use of simple graphics to make short games is a fun way to learn programming constructs and is especially good for visual learners.

What this book covers

Chapter 1, Welcome! Let's Get Started, discusses Python and setting up a Python development environment on Windows, Mac, and Linux operating systems.

Chapter 2, Variables, Functions, and Users, covers Python data types and functions, as well as how to program Python to get information from the user, store that information, and use it later.

Chapter 3, Calculate This!, uses Python to make a calculator that has multiple mathematical functions. We also learn about working in our file structure and the proper way to save code files.

Chapter 4, Making Decisions – Python Control Flows, covers the use of `if`, `elif`, and `else`, as well as the use of `for` and `while` loops, in order to help create programs that make decisions based on user actions.

Chapter 5, *Loops and Logic*, builds upon what we have learned in the previous chapters and allows us to build a number guessing game. We will build easy and difficult versions of the game.

Chapter 6, *Working with Data – Lists and Dictionaries*, explains how to use lists and dictionaries to store data. The differences between lists and dictionaries are explained, and we spend time building small lists and dictionaries as well.

Chapter 7, *What's in Your Backpack?*, allows us to use functions, loops, logic, lists and dictionaries to build a different kind of guessing game. We will also learn about nesting dictionaries and lists.

Chapter 8, *pygame*, talks about a popular graphical library that is used in Python to make small games. We will learn the fundamental aspects of this library and experiment with some code.

Chapter 9, *Tiny Tennis*, this game is a clone of a popular game. We will re-create the game using all of the skills that we have learned throughout the book. This is the major project of the book.

Chapter 10, *Keep Coding!*, shows you all the opportunities that will arise once you read this book.

Appendix, *Quick Task Answers*, has the answers to all the quick task questions within the chapters.

What you need for this book

This book can be used with Windows 10, Mac OS X, or Ubuntu Linux operating systems. Other versions of these operating systems may work; however, this book has been written specifically to address these systems. Additionally, you will need the Internet to download some tools, such as recommended text editors, for your operating system. All recommended downloads are open source.

Who this book is for

This book is for kids who are ready to move from graphically-based programming environments, such as Scratch, and into text-based environments. Kids who are ready to create their own projects will engage with this book, especially those who have played games. No prior programming experience is needed to complete the projects in this book; this book is for kids aged 10 years and above, who are ready to learn about Python programming.

Conventions

In this book, you will find a number of text styles that distinguish between different kinds of information. Here are some examples of these styles and an explanation of their meaning.

Code words in text, database table names, folder names, filenames, file extensions, pathnames, dummy URLs, user input, and Twitter handles are shown as follows: "Why don't you try giving the computer the `name` variable with your name and then the `height` variable with your height?"

A block of code is set as follows:

```
def name():
    first_name = input('What is your first name?')
    print('So nice to meet you, ' + first_name)

name()
```

Any command-line input or output is written as follows:

python

>>>print("Hello, world!")

> Warnings or important notes appear in a box like this.

> Tips and tricks appear like this.

Reader feedback

Feedback from our readers is always welcome. Let us know what you think about this book—what you liked or disliked. Reader feedback is important for us as it helps us develop titles that you will really get the most out of.

To send us general feedback, simply e-mail feedback@packtpub.com, and mention the book's title in the subject of your message.

If there is a topic that you have expertise in and you are interested in either writing or contributing to a book, see our author guide at www.packtpub.com/authors.

Customer support

Now that you are the proud owner of a Packt book, we have a number of things to help you to get the most from your purchase.

Downloading the example code

You can download the example code files for this book from your account at `http://www.packtpub.com`. If you purchased this book elsewhere, you can visit `http://www.packtpub.com/support` and register to have the files e-mailed directly to you.

You can download the code files by following these steps:

1. Log in or register to our website using your e-mail address and password.
2. Hover the mouse pointer on the **SUPPORT** tab at the top.
3. Click on **Code Downloads & Errata**.
4. Enter the name of the book in the **Search** box.
5. Select the book for which you're looking to download the code files.
6. Choose from the drop-down menu where you purchased this book from.
7. Click on **Code Download**.

You can also download the code files by clicking on the **Code Files** button on the book's webpage at the Packt Publishing website. This page can be accessed by entering the book's name in the **Search** box. Please note that you need to be logged in to your Packt account.

Once the file is downloaded, please make sure that you unzip or extract the folder using the latest version of:

- WinRAR / 7-Zip for Windows
- Zipeg / iZip / UnRarX for Mac
- 7-Zip / PeaZip for Linux

Downloading the color images of this book

We also provide you with a PDF file that has color images of the screenshots/ diagrams used in this book. The color images will help you better understand the changes in the output. You can download this file from `http://www.packtpub.com/sites/default/files/downloads/PythonProjectsforKids_ColorImages.pdf`.

Errata

Although we have taken every care to ensure the accuracy of our content, mistakes do happen. If you find a mistake in one of our books—maybe a mistake in the text or the code—we would be grateful if you could report this to us. By doing so, you can save other readers from frustration and help us improve subsequent versions of this book. If you find any errata, please report them by visiting `http://www.packtpub.com/submit-errata`, selecting your book, clicking on the **Errata Submission Form** link, and entering the details of your errata. Once your errata are verified, your submission will be accepted and the errata will be uploaded to our website or added to any list of existing errata under the Errata section of that title.

To view the previously submitted errata, go to `https://www.packtpub.com/books/content/support` and enter the name of the book in the search field. The required information will appear under the **Errata** section.

Piracy

Piracy of copyrighted material on the Internet is an ongoing problem across all media. At Packt, we take the protection of our copyright and licenses very seriously. If you come across any illegal copies of our works in any form on the Internet, please provide us with the location address or website name immediately so that we can pursue a remedy.

Please contact us at `copyright@packtpub.com` with a link to the suspected pirated material.

We appreciate your help in protecting our authors and our ability to bring you valuable content.

Questions

If you have a problem with any aspect of this book, you can contact us at `questions@packtpub.com`, and we will do our best to address the problem.

1
Welcome! Let's Get Started

If you've picked up this book, then you are taking your first step toward building amazing projects using code. Some of you might want to make games, while others might want to learn more about how all of your favorite websites and apps actually work. If you follow the exercises in this book, you'll be able to do the following:

- Create fun games to play with your family and friends
- Learn about the inner workings of your apps
- Learn how to take charge of your computer

Python projects for you

In this book, you will learn Python code. Specifically, you will learn how to design a computer program from the very beginning. It doesn't matter if you have never coded before because each exercise in this book is designed to get you ready to code. If you have coded before, you will find that this book has some really helpful exercises that can help make your code even better. Additionally, there are some more advanced projects toward the end of the book, which you should definitely take a look at!

What can you do with Python?

If you take a look at the Web and search for Python jobs, you will find that many of the highest paying jobs are in Python. Why?

Python is a very flexible and powerful language in the following ways:

- It can be used in order to go through millions of lines of data
- Python can search for information on a website without having to go to the website itself
- It is even used to host and design websites

So, what will it take to learn Python? If you have never programmed, you will probably want to follow each lesson in order so that you can build the skills you need to make a game or another kind of computer program. The final project in this book will be a game. If you have some other programming experience, such as making modifications to your computer games, using programs such as Scratch or Logo or trying some of the free programming classes on the Internet, then you might decide to skim this book first to see what you already know. It is still recommended that you follow the contents of this book in the order they are presented, as each project builds on the projects that were explained in the previous chapter.

Why you should learn Python

Python teaches all of the basics of an object-oriented programming language, and it is still very powerful. In fact, many Internet companies, most notably Mozilla Firefox and Google, use Python in part or all of their products! Python has also been used to build Django, a free framework to make websites.

It has also been used to build many small video games by people learning about it as well as more advanced programmers. Finally, Python can be used to quickly read and analyze millions of lines of data very quickly! By learning Python, you will be prepared to build a variety of interesting projects, and you will gain the skills necessary to learn other programming languages if you choose to do so.

The prerequisites of Python

Before you get started, you need the following basic materials:

- A computer that can run Windows 7 or higher, Mac OS X 10.6 or higher, or Ubuntu 12.4 or higher. You may also use a Raspberry Pi as it comes preinstalled with Python, pygame, and the other software needed to complete the projects in this book.

- An Internet connection is necessary as some of the software you need to install on your computer might not be installed already. For example, Windows operating systems do not come with Python preinstalled, so an Internet connection will be needed; pygame is also not preinstalled on Windows, Mac, or Linux systems.

- Along with an Internet connection, you will also need a web browser, such as Firefox, Safari, Chrome, or Internet Explorer, which will allow you to visit the Python documentation pages.

All of the code samples in this book are available for download on the Packt Publishing website.

Setting up your computer

There are many different computer operating systems, but the most common operating systems are Macintosh (Mac), Windows, and Linux. You should follow the installation steps that go with your operating system. There are some subtle but important differences between the systems.

For the projects in this book, we will be using Python 2.7. While there are higher versions than this (3.x), these versions do not work dependably with pygame on Windows, Mac, or Ubuntu Linux as yet. However, this book will be written to use conventions that work in both versions of Python so that projects are easily completed on Raspberry Pi (which uses Python 3.x that's been specially configured with pygame) with just a few modifications. These modifications will be duly noted.

For Mac and Ubuntu Linux users

Mac and Linux systems share enough similarities that people who use either Mac or Linux can follow the same set of instructions. These instructions will make note of any differences between Mac and Ubuntu Linux.

Python 2.7

At the time of writing, Mac OS X El Capitan comes with Python 2.7 preinstalled, so nothing extra needs to be done at this point.

Ubuntu Linux 15.10 has Python 2.7.10 installed by default, so users of this latest (as of writing this) version of Linux also need to do nothing extra at this point.

Terminal – the command line and the Python shell

Mac and Ubuntu Linux users have Python by default, but finding Python is tricky if you don't know where to look. There is a program called **Terminal** on both Mac and Linux operating systems. This program allows you to exercise a lot of control over your computer in these ways:

- On a Mac, go to **Finder** | **Applications** | **Utilities** and click on **Terminal**. The terminal application will open up, and you should see a small, white window on your screen.

- Ubuntu users can search for `terminal` on their desktops, and the program will show up in their **Start** menu. When you click on the terminal, you will see a small, black window on your screen.

- The terminal also functions as a Python shell when a command is given to run Python. We will learn about this later.

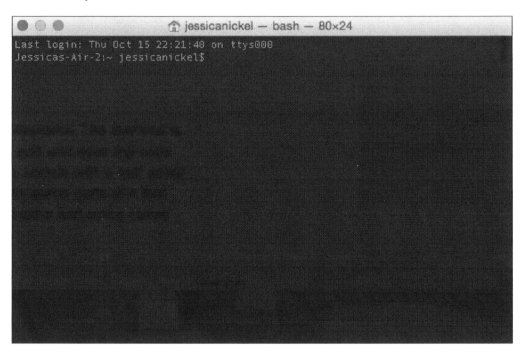

Text editor

A **text** editor is a helpful tool for writing and editing Python programs. The terminal is a nice place to test snippets of Python code, but when we want to edit and save the code in order to use it over again, we will need a text editor. Although both Mac and Linux systems come with a text editor, there are some very nice, free editors that have good features. **jEdit** is one of these editors.

 For Mac and Linux, go to `http://www.jedit.org/` and download jEdit. Follow the installation instructions.

To successfully complete all of the exercises in this book, you will often need to keep both the terminal and text editor open at the same time on your screen.

This is what the text editor application, jEdit, looks like in Mac and Linux:

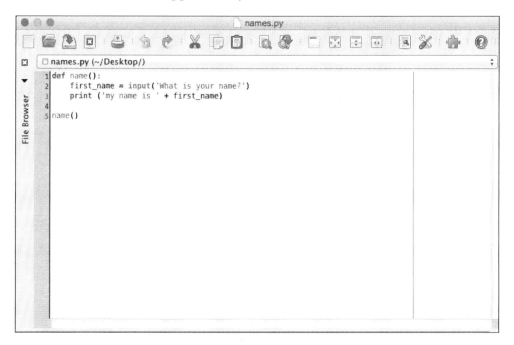

For Windows users

Windows users, this setup might require help from your parents. Since Python is not installed by default on Windows, some system adjustments need to be made to successfully run Python on your computer. If you are feeling uncertain about performing these system changes yourself, make sure to ask for help:

1. First, you will need to download version 2.7.11 of Python.

Use the official Python website for the latest releases for Windows at https://www.python.org/downloads/release/python-2711/.

With Windows, you need to figure out if you are running 32-bit or 64-bit so that you can download the correct version of Python. To help you to determine which one is correct, visit

http://windows.microsoft.com/en-gb/windows/32-bit-and-64-bit-windows#1TC=windows-7.

Download *x86only* if your computer is running 32-bit Windows. Most users will download the x86-64 version of Python.

2. Choose the executable installer, and you will see the download progress.

3. When the download is complete, you will see a prompt to run Python. Click on **Run**.

4. An install prompt will come up, and when it does, look at the bottom of the window and click on the box next to **Add Python 2.x to Path**. Then, select **Install Now**.

5. Follow the installation instructions. Each step may take a few minutes. Once the installation is done, you will have an icon for Python 2.7.11, which you can find by searching for Python in the Windows search bar. This will open a special Python shell from where you can run and test the Python code.

Command prompt

In Windows 10, you will see a terminal called the **command prompt**. The command prompt is significantly different in Windows than it is on Mac or Linux.

To find the command prompt in Windows 10, perform these steps:

1. Go to the search bar at the bottom of the screen and search for cmd or command.

2. When you do, you will see the command prompt desktop app appear. Click on this app to open the command prompt, which looks like this:

Text editor

In Windows, Notepad is the default text editor. However, **Notepad++** is a much better substitute.

To get Notepad++, perform these steps:

1. Go to `https://notepad-plus-plus.org/` and download the latest version.
2. Once the program has been downloaded, click on **Run**.

Notepad++ looks like this:

Write and run your first program in the command line

Now that you are set up, it is time to write your first line of code in Python! This line of code is almost a tradition for people who are programming for the first time, and it allows us to use one of the most basic, but most useful, functions in the Python language.

First, you need to start running a Python shell. On Mac or Linux, open your terminal and type this:

```
python
```

In the Mac or Ubuntu terminal, your resulting Python shell will look like this:

```
>>>
```

In Windows, type `Python` in the search bar at the bottom of the page. Then, select Python 2.7.11 from your apps. You will also have a Python shell open:

```
>>>
```

Once you see this symbol, your computer is now ready to work with the Python code. In your terminal or IDLE, type the following:

```
>>>print("Hello, world!")
```

Once you have typed this, double-check to make sure that all of the spaces are exactly as they've been written. In Python, every space actually matters. Every punctuation mark matters. Once you have checked your code, hit *Enter*.

What is your result or the output of your code? If the output looks like the following image, then great! You typed all of your code properly so the computer will understand what you want it to do. The expected output will be similar to what is shown here:

```
😣 ● ⊟   jess@jess-VirtualBox: ~
jess@jess-VirtualBox:~$ python
Python 2.7.10 (default, Oct 14 2015, 16:09:02)
[GCC 5.2.1 20151010] on linux2
Type "help", "copyright", "credits" or "license" for more information.
>>> print('Hello, world!')
Hello, world!
>>>
```

For Windows users, the output window will look like this:

```
C:\Python27\python.exe
Python 2.7.11 (v2.7.11:6d1b6a68f775, Dec  5 2015, 20:40:30) [MSC v.1500 64 bit (AMD64)] on win32
Type "help", "copyright", "credits" or "license" for more information.
>>> print('Hello, world!')
Hello, world!
>>>
```

So, if your output does not look like the preceding code, you need to figure out what's wrong with it. Here are some of the reasons for this:

- Did you make a typing error?
- Did you forget to use parenthesis or round brackets () for the words `'Hello, world!'`?
- Did you forget to use the `' '` single quotation marks for `Hello, world!`?

If you still have a problem, compare your code to the sample input code and fix any mistakes. Then, try to run the code again.

Python is what is called a *case-sensitive* language. Python cares about uppercase, lowercase, and whitespace. You need to watch what you type. You might get some strange messages from your computer if you make a typing mistake or a syntax error.

Make yourself a work folder

Before we get started on any large projects, we need to make a work folder. In the next chapter, you will start writing whole files of code that need to be run; therefore, we will need a place to put those files. Since you are setting up now, let's make a folder.

If you are very good at getting around your computer, you can put your folder wherever you want to.

If you are not too good at getting around your computer, you will probably want to put your folder on your desktop.

On both Mac and Windows machines, you can right-click somewhere on your desktop wallpaper, and a box will pop up with several options. One of the options will say **New**, and when you hover over **New**, you will get several other options. Choose **New Folder**, and a new folder icon will appear on your desktop. It will be named `untitled`, so you should give it a better name.

To find your folder in the Mac or Linux terminals, respectively, open one of them and perform these steps:

1. Run the `cd ..` command until you are at the root, which is often the name you have given to your computer. You may need to run the command three or four times.

2. Now, you will be able to run python programs by typing `python3.5program.py`.

To find your folder in the Windows command line, open the command prompt and perform these steps:

1. Run the `cd ..`command until you are at the root or `C:\>`. You may need to run the command three or four times.

2. Now, you will be able to run Python programs by typing `python program.py`.

A quick task for you

Now that you have finished this chapter, can you answer these questions?

Q1. What is a terminal (Mac/Linux) or command prompt (Windows)?

1. A terminal is used to put data into or get data out of a computer without using the icons on the desktop.
2. A terminal can be used to write computer programs.
3. A terminal can be used to do complex work, such as giving hints on Python code.
4. A terminal can do all of the above.

Q2. When you first open the terminal/command prompt, what do you need to do so that you can start reading and writing the Python code?

1. Start typing the code.
2. Type the word `python`.
3. Wait for Python to start.
4. None of the above; do something different.

Q3. How is the Python shell different from the command line?

1. They are exactly the same.
2. The command line cannot run Python commands.
3. The Python shell is started by typing the word `python` into the command line.
4. The Python shell can be used to test lines of Python code.

 Compare your answers with those you find at the back of the book.

Summary

If you are reading this, it is because you have made it through some of the tricky work of getting ready to learn to program projects with Python. Congratulations! Setting it up is always tough. Hopefully, you learned a bit more about the tools on your computer, such as the text editor and terminal that every programmer uses to do their daily work. Also, you learned about the Python `print()` function, and you should now be able to print out messages in your Python shell. The fun is just beginning as we have so much more to learn!

In the next chapter, you will learn about the building blocks of Python programs. We'll start with variables and learn about all the different kinds of information we can put in them. Then, we will build some functions that put these variables together and help us make blocks of code that have special jobs. Finally, we will even learn how to make a computer ask a user questions and store their answers so that our programs can become interactive!

2

Variables, Functions, and Users

In the previous chapter, you learned how to install Python on your computer. You also learned how to use the `print` statement in Python and printed some messages using your Python shell. We are now going to jump into a lot of details so that we can build our first project together. It will include the following:

- Variables
- Variable names
- Strings, integers, and floats
- Functions

Variables

A variable is when one letter or word is used to represent a different letter, word, number, or value. One way to think of a variable is to imagine that you are programming a computer so that it can make memories. For example, my name is Jessica. If I am writing a computer program and I want that program to remember my name, I will assign my name to a variable. This will look like `name = 'Jessica'`. The variable is `name`. `Jessica` in the memory.

Perhaps I would like the computer to remember something else about me as well. Maybe I want the computer program to remember that I am 64 inches, or roughly 128 cm, tall. I will say `height_inches = 64` or `height_centimeters = 128`. The variables here are `height_inches` and `height_centimeters`. The memories are my height in inches and my height in centimeters.

Why don't you try giving a computer the `name` variable with your name and then a `height` variable with your height?

First, open your Python shell and type the following code:

```
name = 'yourname'
height = 'your height'
```

Now that the variables are stored, you can type `print(name)` or `print(height)`. Since you created a memory for the computer with your name and your height, the computer will print the memory that you gave it. If you take a look at the screenshot from my Python shell, you will see that the computer printed the memories that I assigned it. Notice that we do not use single quotes around the variable names:

```
Last login: Tue Oct 13 21:25:04 on ttys001
Jessicas-Air-2:~ jessicanickel$ python
Python 2.7.8 (default, Jul  2 2014, 10:14:46)
[GCC 4.2.1 Compatible Apple LLVM 5.1 (clang-503.0.40)] on darwin
Type "help", "copyright", "credits" or "license" for more information.
>>>
>>> name = "Jessica"
>>> height_inches = 64
>>> height_centimeters = 128
>>>
>>> print(name)
Jessica
>>>
>>> print(height_inches)
64
>>>
>>> print(height_centimeters)
128
>>> ▊
```

If the values, or memories, that you assigned to the variables are printed in your Python terminal, then it is perfect. If not, you may have an error. There are a lot of reasons due to which an error can occur. You may have typed your variable name or your information in a way that breaks the Python convention. Some common errors include using capital letters.

Naming variables – conventions to follow

There are some conventions that are used to name variables in Python. It might seem silly to have guidelines about naming things, but following the conventions is really important because it helps other people read your code. Also, the Python shell is designed to work with the conventions.

To avoid errors, your variable names should use lowercase letters. If your variable uses more than one word, such as the `height_inches` variable, then it should have underscores to connect the words together.

If you use two words to name your variable and do not connect them with an underscore, you will get an error. Take a look at the following screenshot and see where it says `SyntaxError: invalid syntax`. Notice this error occurred because the `height centimeters` variable did not have an underscore to connect the words:

```
Last login: Tue Oct 13 21:31:03 on ttys000
Jessicas-Air-2:~ jessicanickel$ python
Python 2.7.8 (default, Jul  2 2014, 10:14:46)
[GCC 4.2.1 Compatible Apple LLVM 5.1 (clang-503.0.40)] on darwin
Type "help", "copyright", "credits" or "license" for more information.
>>>
>>>
>>> height centimeters = 64
  File "<stdin>", line 1
    height centimeters = 64
                   ^
SyntaxError: invalid syntax
>>> █
```

What can variables remember?

Python variables can be programmed to remember all kinds of information! You will notice in our original example that we stored a word and then a number. There are three different kinds of information that we will be using to build our calculator in *Chapter 3, Calculate This!*, strings, integers, and floats. Each bit of information is input and output a little differently.

Strings

In Python, a string is any piece of data that's captured between two single quote marks, that is, these symbols ' '. Sometimes, double quotation marks are used. For example, I can have a string variable that looks like this:

```
sentence = 'This is a sentence about Python.'
```

This string variable contains letters and words. Most string variables do. However, you can store a number as a string also as long as that number is in single quotes:

```
number_string = '40'
```

If we can store all kinds of information as strings, why do we need other data types? Well, when we store numbers as strings, we cannot do math with the numbers! Type this problem into your Python shell, and then you will see why we need data types besides strings:

```
first_number = '10'
second_number = '20'
print(first_number + second_number)
```

What happened in your Python shell? You might have expected the printed output to be 30 since 10 plus 20 is equal to 30. However, Python saw each number as a text string and simply put the two text strings next to each other. So, your result was probably 1020. Here is how this looks in the Python shell:

```
Last login: Tue Oct 13 21:36:31 on ttys001
Jessicas-Air-2:~ jessicanickel$ python
Python 2.7.8 (default, Jul  2 2014, 10:14:46)
[GCC 4.2.1 Compatible Apple LLVM 5.1 (clang-503.0.40)] on darwin
Type "help", "copyright", "credits" or "license" for more information.
>>>
>>>
>>>
>>> first_number = "10"
>>> second_number = "20"
>>> print(first_number + second_number)
1020
>>>
```

Integers

Computers are really great at math, and math will allow us to execute more complicated programs, such as games. Python stores whole number data as integers.

Let's start with integers:

- An integer is simply a plain whole number. If we want to make our variables store integers, we would take away the quotes.
- Then, when we add the two variables and print the output, we will get a mathematical result.

Try it out! Let's do some math with these variables:

1. Type the following two variables in your Python shell:

   ```
   first_number = 10
   second_number = 20
   ```

2. Then, print the output by typing print and the variables:

   ```
   print(first_number + second_number)
   ```

After completing step 2, press *Enter*. Your result should be 30. This is because Python is reading the numbers as integers, and Python understands integers with mathematical operators. In fact, Python understands math so well that you will notice that no equals sign was needed to tell Python to output the answer. Take a look at this screenshot:

```
Last login: Tue Oct 13 21:39:35 on ttys000
Jessicas-Air-2:~ jessicanickel$ python
Python 2.7.8 (default, Jul  2 2014, 10:14:46)
[GCC 4.2.1 Compatible Apple LLVM 5.1 (clang-503.0.40)] on darwin
Type "help", "copyright", "credits" or "license" for more information.
>>>
>>>
>>> first_number = 10
>>> second_number = 20
>>> print(first_number + second_number)
30
>>>
```

Floating point numbers (floats)

Hopefully, you now better understand how Python works with integers (whole numbers). However, people and computers often need to work in fractional numbers. In Python, these numbers are called **floating point numbers**, but many people call them *floats* as a shortcut:

- Floats are actually a really fancy way of saying *numbers using decimals*

- Floats are called this because the decimal point can be anywhere among the numbers, allowing for decimals of many different sizes

- Setting numbers as floats allows us to do more complicated math using fractional numbers

- To set a variable to a float, you don't have to do anything special or different from what you did to set the integers

- Python knows that a number input (a variable, for example) with a decimal point is a float, and Python will output the answers as a float if the problem is clear

In your Python shell, try this math problem using floating point numbers instead of integers:

```
first_number = 10.3
second_number = 20.3
print(first_number + second_number)
```

This time, in your Python shell, you should notice that Python recognized the variable input as floating point numbers and was able to output the complete and correct answer without us having to use additional instructions. The output from your `print` statement should be `30.6`, as you can see in this screenshot of the Python shell:

```
Last login: Tue Oct 13 21:41:30 on ttys001
Jessicas-Air-2:~ jessicanickel$ python
Python 2.7.8 (default, Jul  2 2014, 10:14:46)
[GCC 4.2.1 Compatible Apple LLVM 5.1 (clang-503.0.40)] on darwin
Type "help", "copyright", "credits" or "license" for more information.
>>>
>>>
>>> first_number = 10.3
>>> second_number = 20.3
>>> print(first_number + second_number)
30.6
>>>
>>> 
```

Combining strings, integers, and floats

So far, we have only attempted to combine items that share a data type. We have added two strings, two integers, or two floats. What happens when you try to add two different types of information, such as a string and an integer? In your Python shell, type the following lines of code and pay attention to the output:

```
first_number = '10'
second_number = 20
print(first_number + second_number)
```

You are likely to notice the error that you receive. The important line to pay attention to is `TypeError: cannot concatenate 'str' and 'int' objects`. Python is telling us that it cannot work with these two different data types and that makes sense. So, if you do make a mistake in your typing or try to execute an operation in two different data types, you may get an error like this:

```
Last login: Tue Oct 13 21:43:09 on ttys001
Jessicas-Air-2:~ jessicanickel$ python
Python 2.7.8 (default, Jul  2 2014, 10:14:46)
[GCC 4.2.1 Compatible Apple LLVM 5.1 (clang-503.0.40)] on darwin
Type "help", "copyright", "credits" or "license" for more information.
>>>
>>> first_number = "10"
>>> second_number = 20
>>> print(first_number + second_number)
Traceback (most recent call last):
  File "<stdin>", line 1, in <module>
TypeError: cannot concatenate 'str' and 'int' objects
>>> 
```

Functions

Once we have variables, we can use them to do some pretty interesting things. The most interesting thing is to build functions. Python functions are blocks of code that we can build to do a specific job. We build these functions once, and then we can reuse them in our code just by typing the name. This is really helpful. For example, if I need to write a program that adds two numbers (a calculator, for example), I do not want to have to write three or four lines of code every time I want to add two numbers. Instead, I want to write one function that can add two numbers together, and then use that single line whenever I need to add numbers.

Before we begin building functions of our own, we need to also know that Python has a lot of amazing functions that are built in. Some of Python's functions are things we will use all the time. Others we won't talk about in this book, but as you become a more skilled programmer, you will learn more about Python's built-in functions.

Built-in functions

Here's something about some built-in functions and what they do:

- `int()`: This converts a string or a float into an integer
- `float()`: This converts a string or an integer into a float
- `raw_input()`: This gets information from a user and stores it in the computer to use later
- `str()`: This converts an integer, float, or other information into a string
- `help()`: This provides access to Python's help

We will be using these functions to help us build our first project in the next chapter.

 If you are curious about what other functions are built in or if you want to know more, you can go to the Python documents at `https://docs.python.org/2.7/library/functions.html?highlight=built%20functions#`.

Initially, the documents can seem overwhelming because they are very detailed. The detail can make the documents difficult to understand at times, but the documents are very helpful and are used by many programmers.

Parts of a function

There are basic parts to think about when you want to build your own function. First, here's the basic function to add two numbers:

```python
def addition():
    first_number = 30
    second_number = 60
    print(first_number + second_number)
```

The first line of this code is new, so we need to understand what it means:

- The first thing to notice is the word `def`. In Python, this is short for define, and it is used to define a new function.

- The next thing to notice is the name of the function. The name of the function has the same guidelines as the names of variables. A function needs to use lowercase letters, and when it has many words, there need to be underscores between each word.

- After the name of the `addition()` function, you will notice the parentheses `()`. These are empty in this function, but sometimes they are not empty. Even if they are, the parentheses must *ALWAYS* be a part of the function that you create.

- Finally, the first line of the function ends with a colon. The colon (`:`), ends the first line of the function.

A function can be short, such as this `addition()` function, which is only four lines in total, or it can be really long. Every line after the first line in a Python function needs to be indented using spaces. When we work on building our own functions in the next section of this chapter, you will learn how to make indents in your Python shell. We will also discuss proper spacing in the text editor.

There are a lot of new details to remember in order to write a function. What happens if you forget a detail? If you forget to indent a line, Python will let you know and output an error. Your function will not run, and your code will not work. Python's use of indentation is known as **whitespace**, and there are rules about whitespace use in Python.

By now, you are very familiar with doing additions in Python, so we will keep working with the addition code. There are special considerations in order to write functions in the Python shell. Because a function is a block of code, we want to follow these guidelines when we are trying to perform functions in the shell:

- After you type the first line and press *Enter*, make sure you press *Tab* before you type each line
- When you have completed typing all the lines, hit *Enter* twice so that the Python shell knows that you are done creating the function

In your Python shell, type the `addition()` function exactly as it appears here:

```
def addition():
  first_number = 30
  second_number = 60
  print(first_number + second_number)
```

Notice how the function looks in the Python shell:

```
Jessicas-Air-2:~ jessicanickel$ python
Python 2.7.8 (default, Jul  2 2014, 10:14:46)
[GCC 4.2.1 Compatible Apple LLVM 5.1 (clang-503.0.40)] on darwin
Type "help", "copyright", "credits" or "license" for more information.
>>>
>>>
>>> def addition():
...     first_number = 30
...     second_number = 60
...     print(first_number + second_number)
...
>>>
>>>
```

Now that you have typed your function, you need to learn how to use the function. To use the function in the Python shell, type the name of the function and the parentheses:

```
addition()
```

Typing the function is also known as calling the function. When you call the `addition()` function in the Python shell and then press *Enter*, you will get an output as the answer to the problem. Notice how this is displayed here:

```
Jessicas-Air-2:~ jessicanickel$ python
Python 2.7.8 (default, Jul  2 2014, 10:14:46)
[GCC 4.2.1 Compatible Apple LLVM 5.1 (clang-503.0.40)] on darwin
Type "help", "copyright", "credits" or "license" for more information.
>>>
>>>
>>> def addition():
...     first_number = 30
...     second_number = 60
...     print(first_number + second_number)
...
>>>
>>>
>>> addition()
90
>>>
```

Compare your result to the results shown in the preceding screenshots. Once you know that your function runs the way you want it to, you can show it to your parents and friends by asking them to look at your code. It is a good idea to test your function by retyping it with different numbers.

Users interacting with your program

We just built a function that adds two numbers together. Learning to make a program that does math is interesting, but our function is limited because our `addition()` function needs to have variables changed manually to calculate results for different numbers.

What if there was a way to get information from the user and store *THAT* information in a variable so that it could be used by addition or subtraction functions each time? Anyone who has used a calculator of any kind already knows that this is possible. Python has a function called `raw_input()` that allows us to tell the program to ask the user a question. The `raw_input()` function is incredibly useful. We can get every kind of information from the user this way, and we can make interactions between the user and the computer based on the user input.

We can use the Python shell to test how the `raw_input()` function works. Try typing these two lines of code into your Python shell:

```
name = raw_input('What is your name?')
print(name)
```

What happened here? Let's have a look:

- What should have happened is that you should have had a prompt in the terminal that asked `'What is your name?'` Then, you can type your response.

- Following your response, hit *Enter*. Nothing will happen (nothing should happen yet!).

- You have given the computer information (a memory) to store in the `name` variable, but now you need to get the information out of the `name` variable.

- You can get the output of the memory that the user entered by printing the `name` variable.

In this screenshot, you can see the entire sequence in the Python shell:

```
Last login: Tue Oct 13 22:24:47 on ttys001
Jessicas-Air-2:~ jessicanickel$ python3.5
Python 3.5.0 (v3.5.0:374f501f4567, Sep 12 2015, 11:00:19)
[GCC 4.2.1 (Apple Inc. build 5666) (dot 3)] on darwin
Type "help", "copyright", "credits" or "license" for more information.
>>>
>>>
>>> name = input("What is your name?")
What is your name?Jessica
>>> print(name)
Jessica
>>>
```

Using the text editor and the command line

So far, we have used the Python shell to write and test code. The shell is great because we type a line of code or even a few lines of code, and then we run them immediately to see whether they work. However, you may have noticed that there isn't a way to save any of the code that we write.

For a program to run, it needs to have all of the code available. Using a text editor is just like writing a report, an email, or a paper: we write our code and save it; then, we go back to edit it if we want to. In order to make Python use and understand our file, we need to use the command line and tell Python to run the file.

To perform our next task as well as the remaining tasks in the book, we will use our text editor side by side with our terminal/command prompt. Let's walk through the setup of the text editor and command line right now.

The first thing you need to do is as follows:

- Make a special folder where you can store your code files, and remember how to find this folder! (Look back at *Chapter 1, Welcome! Let's Get Started*, for instructions.)

- This folder, or directory, is very important, as it will be the place where you put the work that you create for the rest of this book

- Python needs to be able to access this directory to run all the programs, and soon, we will write files that will use other files; so, all of the files need to live in the same place

Once you are certain that you have a special work folder, you can open the text editor program we set up in *Chapter 1, Welcome! Let's Get Started*. You will also open a new window in a terminal or in the command prompt.

Build your own function – name()

So, you have learned about variables and how they store information. You have also learned about how these variables can be used inside of a function. Finally, you have learned how to use special Python functions, such as input(), to help get information from users and store it in the computer. You are ready to build your own function using variables and input().

Set up your project file

The function that we will build now is called name(). The purpose of this function will be to ask the user their name, store (remember) the name, and then print out a friendly message to the user.

To start this function, do the following:

1. Open a new file in your text editor.
2. Go to **Save** and name the file name.py.

 You need to use .py at the end of all of your code files so that the files run in the terminal/command prompt. Python only recognizes .py files.

3. Save the file in the folder you made for all of your Python work.

Begin your project

Once you have set up a project file, the first thing you might want to do is add a short comment to your file. A comment allows humans to quickly understand what is happening in the code. Whenever you are writing something that is not code, you should start the line with a hashtag, or hash. The hash is one way to tell the computer, *Ignore this!*, yet it allows humans to read the text. Type the following line in your file:

```
# This is my first function called name. It will ask the name and
# print a message.
```

Writing code

The next line you type will begin the computer-readable code. First, make sure that there is a space between the comment you wrote and the first line of computer-readable code. As we learned earlier, you will start the function using the Python word `def`. Then, you will type one space and the name of the function:

```
def name
```

Next, you will add parentheses `()` and a colon `:` to the first line:

```
def name():
```

Now, it is time to go to the next line. For the next line, you will need to indent. Use the spacebar to insert four spaces. In Python, spaces matter. Using the *Tab* key, or mixing between tab and space, is a problem in Python and causes errors.

Since we are asking the user for their first name, you can use the words `first_name` for the variable if you like:

```
def name():
    first_name =
```

The `first_name` variable will store the answer to the question, `What is your first name?` Remember, though, we have to use the `raw_input()` function to get the user to answer the question! So, we will add the `raw_input()` function and question to the code:

```
def name():
    first_name = input('What is your first name?')
```

So far, we have programmed a way for the computer to ask the user for their first name, and we have made a variable called `first_name` to remember the string of information.

Even though we have a file that has some lines of code, if we were to run our code right now, nothing at all would happen. We need a way to show the user their name, and it would be even nicer if we sent the user a welcoming message. We need to write the code for program output.

We have been using `print` to output our information from *Chapter 1, Welcome! Let's Get Started*, and throughout this chapter, and `print` is also useful here. We can tell our function to print the `first_name` information, and we can put that together with a nice message. Add this line to your code:

```
print('So nice to meet you, ' + first_name)
```

Your total code for the `name()` function should look like this:

```
def name():
    first_name = input('What is your first name?')
    print('So nice to meet you, ' + first_name)
```

Here is a sample of how the program looks in a text editor:

```
1  #This is my first function called name. It will ask the name and
2  #print a message.
3
4  def name():
5      first_name = input('What is your first name?')
6      print('So nice to meet you, ' + first_name)
```

We need only to add the final line of code, which is to call the `name()` function. If we do not call the function, it will not run. To call the function, you should leave an empty line after `print`, and on a new line, unindent and type `name()`. Take a look at this code sample, and add the `name()` function to your code:

```
def name():
    first_name = input('What is your first name?')
    print('So nice to meet you, ' + first_name)


name()
```

Now that we have created this function, we can use it to greet anybody because the user is telling us each time what `first_name` should be. We have made a reusable block of code.

Running your program

Now you have to save your work:

1. Go to the **Save** option in your text editor and save the work for name.py.

2. Once you have saved this work, you should go to your terminal/command prompt.

3. Make sure that you are in the correct folder.

 If you are not sure, you can type pwd (Mac/Linux) or echo %cd% (Windows) to find out what folder you are in.

4. When you are in the same folder as your work, type:

    python name.py

5. Then, press *Enter*. Your program should begin to run.

Once you type in the name, the output should look like this:

Python	bash

```
Last login: Wed Oct 14 21:56:40 on ttys001
Jessicas-Air-2:~ jessicanickel$ cd Documents
Jessicas-Air-2:Documents jessicanickel$ python3.5 name.py
What is your first name? Jessica
So nice to meet you,  Jessica
```

You now have a program to share with family and friends that will seem amazing, especially if they have never programmed before!

Going the extra mile

So, if you really want to understand all of this, go the extra mile! Experiment with the code that you just created so that you can see what works and what does not work. If you get a strange error, you can always copy and paste the error into an Internet search engine; most of the errors we've taken a look at so far have happened to other people. Here are some tips to help you experiment and gain mastery:

*   Change the input question
*   Change the message to the user
*   Change the function name

- Change the variable name
- Add a second variable and a second input question
- Add the second variable to the output question

A quick task for you

Now that you have finished this chapter, can you answer these questions?

Q1. What must a function begin with?

1. def
2. Function
3. Input
4. Whitespace

Q2. What are conventions that are used to name variables and functions?

1. Must use lowercase letters
2. Multiple words need to be connected with underscores
3. Cannot use a number to start a name
4. All of the above

Q3. Every line after the first line of a function must be?

1. Named using numbers
2. Have a colon, :
3. Indented
4. Use parentheses ()

Q4. If you want a code file to run in Python, you need to end it with?

1. .txt
2. .odt
3. .pdf
4. .py

Q5. To run a code file in the terminal, what do you need to do?

1. Type the name of the file in the terminal
2. Type the name of the file in the terminal while running Python
3. In the correct folder, type Python and the name of the file
4. All of the above steps in order

Summary

In this chapter, we learned how to store information in variables so that a computer could remember it later. We learned how to use variables to make a function that could add two preprogrammed numbers together. Then, things got interesting when we learned how to make the computer ask questions and remember the user's answers! Using `raw_input()`, we learned how to store answers as variables to use later in the `name()` function that we built together. We started saving our work in `.py` files so that we could run and rerun our files in our terminal/command prompt without having to retype the files all the time.

In the next chapter, you will build a four-function calculator to run in the command line using all of the skills you learned in this chapter!

3
Calculate This!

In the previous chapter, you learned about the uses of variables, different data types, and functions. You created your own function and learned how to get basic information from a user with the `raw_input()` function. Using these building blocks, you can begin to design basic programs.

The first program we make will be a five-function calculator that calculates two numbers as input. The calculator will help us learn to understand the mathematical functions that are a part of Python, which will be useful for our game at the end of the book. In addition to this, this calculator will form the foundation for a more complex calculator in *Chapter 5, Loops and Logic.*

The calculator

The first calculator was invented in 1966 at Texas Instruments (`http://www.ti.com/corp/docs/company/history/timeline/eps/1960/docs/67-handheld_calc_invented.htm`) and was able to do addition, subtraction, multiplication, and division. The calculator had eighteen keys and could display twelve numbers on the screen. While it doesn't seem like much at first, especially compared to the technology we now enjoy, there is quite a lot of code and decision making that go into the operations that a basic calculator performs.

When we want to figure out how something works, we need to break it down into smaller parts. Let's take a look at how the calculator adds numbers together:

1. First, the calculator needs power.
2. The user enters the first number.
3. The user presses an operation key (+, -, *, or /).
4. The user enters a second number.
5. The user presses the = key.
6. Then, an answer is printed to the screen.

On a basic calculator, the computer does not keep all of the numbers on the screen. The computer must store the first number that the user entered in its memory.

We will run our first calculator program inside of the terminal/command prompt, so there are other things we must consider in addition to how the numbers will be stored. For example:

- How will we prompt the user to get the information that we need?
- What happens if the user enters a text string instead of integers or floats?
- What happens if the user enters numbers as a string instead of as integers or floats?

These are just some of the logical questions that need to be considered as we plan how to write our own calculator program. Can you think of any other problems that need to be solved?

Basic functions

We learned at the beginning of this chapter that the first electronic calculator had four basic functions: addition, subtraction, multiplication, and division. We will be working on programming each of these functions, and we will also learn a fifth mathematical function that we can program for our calculator called modulo.

Through the beginning of this chapter, we will use the `addition()` function as our example. Once we have created and tested an `addition()` function that does what we want it to, we will then build our other functions.

Let's return to our example of the addition function in *Chapter 2, Variables, Functions, and Users*. Recall how we programmed this function:

```
Jessicas-Air-2:~ jessicanickel$ python
Python 2.7.8 (default, Jul  2 2014, 10:14:46)
[GCC 4.2.1 Compatible Apple LLVM 5.1 (clang-503.0.40)] on darwin
Type "help", "copyright", "credits" or "license" for more information.
>>>
>>>
>>> def addition():
...     first_number = 30
...     second_number = 60
...     print(first_number + second_number)
...
>>>
>>>
```

The addition function in the preceding screenshot does perform proper addition and prints the answer. However, there are problems with designing an `addition()` function this way. One problem is that the program can only add the same two numbers over and over again. Another problem is that, in this program, we are only using one mathematical operation (addition). This `addition()` function is too inflexible on its own; we need to design a function that is more user friendly.

To design a better mathematical function, we need to solve the problem of user-inputs by letting the user change the numbers in the calculation. We also need to design a calculator where the user has mathematical functions other than addition that can be performed.

Operations on two numbers

We are going to use the `raw_input()` function that we learned about in *Chapter 2, Variables, Functions, and Users*. Recall that from this chapter, we cannot perform addition on two strings. In fact, we cannot perform any kind of mathematical operations on strings.

The following code asks for user input and stores the input in the computer as strings. Type the following code in your Python shell to take a look at the results:

```
def addition():
    first = raw_input('I will add two numbers. Enter the first number')
    second = raw_input('Now enter the second number.')
    print(first + second)
```

What happens when you call the `addition()` function? If you call the `addition()` function, you will see that the addition has *NOT* happened. This program just prints the two numbers together, side by side, in the order that they were entered by the user:

```
Type "help", "copyright", "credits" or "license" for more information.
>>> def addition():
...     first = input('Add two numbers. What is the first number?')
...     second = input('what is the second number?')
...     print(first + second)
...
>>> addition()
Add two numbers. What is the first number?20
what is the second number?30
2030
```

While putting information side by side is useful to combine words into a phrase or sentence, it is not very helpful in performing calculations with numbers, as we discovered in *Chapter 2*, *Variables, Functions, and Users*. Instead, you will want to convert the user's answer to a number so that you can perform mathematical operations on the numbers. To convert the input() function to a number, you will use int() or the float() functions.

Convert data into numbers – int() and float()

In order to change the user data entered in the raw_input() function from a string to a number, we need to use the whole-number-integer, int(), or floating-point-number, float(), functions to make the computer interpret the answer as a number.

Floating point to whole number conversion

To try an example, type the following in your Python shell, and pay attention to the results:

```
a = int(44.5)
b = float(44.5)
print(a)
print(b)
```

In the preceding example, with 44.5, you should notice that the int() function rounds up the number to 44, while the float() function keeps the number at 44.5. This is because int() likes whole numbers and rounds numbers down automatically. Take a look at this screenshot from the Python shell:

```
Jessicas-MacBook-Air-2:~ jessicanickel$ python
Python 2.7.8 (default, Jul  2 2014, 10:14:46)
[GCC 4.2.1 Compatible Apple LLVM 5.1 (clang-503.0.40)] on darwin
Type "help", "copyright", "credits" or "license" for more information.
>>>
>>> def addition():
...     first = raw_input('I will add two numbers. Enter the first number')
...     second = raw_input('Now enter the second number.')
...     print(first + second)
...
>>> addition()
I will add two numbers. Enter the first number20
Now enter the second number.30
2030
>>>
>>>
```

Whole number to floating point conversion

Now, try the reverse. Convert a whole number into an integer and a float using this code in your Python shell:

```
a = int(24)
b = float(24)
print(a)
print(b)
```

In the preceding sample code, you see that the int() function keeps the number at 24, while the float() function adds a decimal place to the number, making it print as 24.0. This is because float is designed to deal with numbers and their decimal places. You can see the results in this screenshot of the Python shell:

```
>>>
>>>
>>>
>>> a = int(24)
>>> b = float(24)
>>> print(a)
24
>>> print(b)
24.0
>>>
>>>
```

Text strings fail in int() and float()

If you try to enter a text string into the int() or float() functions, you will get an error. In fact, you will only be able to type the first line of these two lines into your Python shell. This will immediately evaluate the int('hello') code as an error:

```
int('hello')
float('hello')
```

This happens because int() and float() apply specifically to numbers and do not deal with things that cannot be changed into numbers. In the following screenshot, notice that the Python shell returns something called a traceback with three lines of error code:

```
>>> a = int('hello')
Traceback (most recent call last):
  File "<stdin>", line 1, in <module>
ValueError: invalid literal for int() with base 10: 'hello'
>>>
```

We will switch between using `int()` and `float()` throughout the book so that you become used to using both functions:

- `int()`: This function converts data into a whole number
- `float()`: This function converts data into a number with decimal places

Now that we know about converting strings into numbers, let's rewrite our addition function, get input from the user, and convert the input into decimal numbers using the `float()` function. You can copy this code directly into your text editor:

```
def addition():
    first = float(input('What is your first number?'))
    second = float(input('What is your second number?'))
    print(first + second)
```

In the following screenshot, you see the Python shell with the addition function defined. You also see that when the addition function is called, each `raw_input` line is printed and the user answers by typing in a number. The first and second input have been converted into integers, so when the answer is added together you will notice that the output is now correct according to the standard rules of addition:

```
>>>
>>> def addition():
...     first = int(raw_input('I will add two numbers. Enter the first number'))
...     second = int(raw_input('Now enter the second number.'))
...     print(first + second)
...
>>> addition()
I will add two numbers. Enter the first number44
Now enter the second number.33
77
>>>
```

Creating our first calculator file

Let's save your work before we continue. Open your text editor and make a file called `first_calc.py`, then type the addition function that you just made into that file. Make sure you save the file in your work folder that you made on your desktop back in *Chapter 1, Welcome! Let's Get Started*. It is important to keep your work organized so that you can run your code to test it and show it off:

```
2
3 def addition():
4     first = int(raw_input('What is your first number? '))
5     second = int(raw_input('What is your second number? '))
6     print(first + second)
7
```

New functions – subtraction, multiplication, and division

Now that we have created an `addition()` function that accepts data from the user and converts it into numbers, we are ready to create functions for subtraction, multiplication, and division.

If you are coming back to this after a break, perform the following steps:

1. Open your Python shell so that you can test your code as you write.

2. Next, open your text editor (jEdit in Mac/Linux and Notepad ++ in Windows).

3. Have both windows open on your desktop as you program.

4. When you successfully write and test a line or a few lines of code in the Python shell, copy the lines into your text editor and then *Save Your Work* to the `first_calc.py` file that you created earlier in this chapter.

 Save your work early and as often as you can! Avoid being upset by accidentally erasing your code!

Subtraction

For the next part of our calculator, we will make our subtraction function. We will follow the same prompts as we used for the addition function to create a second function that performs subtraction. In your Python shell, try these steps to create the subtraction function:

1. Type `def` to start your function.

2. Name your function.

3. Add proper syntax, which is parenthesis `()` and `:`.

4. Tab the remaining lines in four spaces each.

5. Request the first number from the user.

6. Request the second number from the user.

7. Print the output using the minus (-) symbol for subtraction.

Once you have tried creating this function in the Python shell, try calling the function using this line of code:

```
subtraction()
```

If the function call works, then you can type your code into your code file exactly as it appears in your Python shell. If your subtraction() function does not run, make sure you did not make any errors when typing your code in the shell. Double-check your code and rerun it until it is smooth. If you are stuck, you can copy the lines of the following code into your Python shell; they will perform subtraction on two integers:

```
def subtraction():
  first = int(raw_input('What is your first number?'))
  second = int(raw_input('What is your second number?'))
  print(first - second)


subtraction()
```

Once you have tested your code in the shell, you can then type it into your text editor. Remember to save your work in your first_calc.py file. Your first_calc.py file should now look something like this:

```
2
3 def addition():
4     first = int(raw_input('What is your first number? '))
5     second = int(raw_input('What is your second number? '))
6     print(first + second)
7
8 def subtraction():
9     first = int(raw_input('What is your first number? '))
10    second = int(raw_input('What is your second number? '))
11    print(first - second)
12
```

Multiplication

By now, you might have observed a pattern in our functions. The multiplication function will follow the same format and logic rules as the addition and subtraction functions. You can continue to ask the user to enter each number, and then the computer will perform a proper calculation.

The following code is for the multiplication function. You can copy it directly, but it is a better idea to try to create the multiplication function on your own. If you try to create your function, you will know how well you have learned the way to create a function. When you are ready, you will see this code for the multiplication function:

```
def multiplication():
    first = int(raw_input('What is your first number?'))
    second = int(raw_input('What is your second number?'))
    print(first * second)
```

Once you have tested your code in your Python shell, remember to type the function in your text editor and save your work in your `first_calc.py` file:

```
3 def addition():
4     first = int(raw_input('What is your first number? '))
5     second = int(raw_input('What is your second number? '))
6     print(first + second)
7
8 def subtraction():
9     first = int(raw_input('What is your first number? '))
10    second = int(raw_input('What is your second number? '))
11    print(first - second)
12
13 def multiplication():
14    first = int(raw_input('What is your first number? '))
15    second = int(raw_input('What is your second number? '))
16    print(first * second)
17
```

Division

Division is the final basic operation that we will program for our first calculator program. As with multiplication, you have already done most of the work for the division part of the calculator. See if you can recall how to create a division function from scratch. Once you have tested your code, compare it to the following code and see if it matches up:

```
def division():
    first = int(raw_input('What is your first number?'))
    second = int(raw_input('What is your second number?'))
    print(first / second)
```

Once you have tested your code, remember to save your work in your `first_calc.py` file:

```
3  def addition():
4      first = int(raw_input('What is your first number? '))
5      second = int(raw_input('What is your second number? '))
6      print(first + second)
7
8  def subtraction():
9      first = int(raw_input('What is your first number? '))
10     second = int(raw_input('What is your second number? '))
11     print(first - second)
12
13 def multiplication():
14     first = int(raw_input('What is your first number? '))
15     second = int(raw_input('What is your second number? '))
16     print(first * second)
17
18 def division():
19     first = int(raw_input('What is your first number? '))
20     second = int(raw_input('What is your second number? '))
21     print(first / second)
22
```

Finding a remainder – modulo

Modulo can seem like a strange concept. In fact, unless you are a programmer, it is likely that you have never heard of modulo. Modulo is a mathematical function that allows us to do a division problem but only return the remainder. Why is this even useful? Why is it a good idea, and why should we care?

Usually, we want to know the entire answer to a division problem—the quotient and the remainder. There are times, though, when we will only want to know the remainder of the division problem. We will only care about what is leftover. Modulo is like a monster eating our dessert: we give the monster numbers to divide, and it just gives us leftovers.

While modulo is not especially useful in the world of school arithmetic, it can be very useful in moving objects in a game. So, it is good for us to build a modulo function and learn how modulo works.

To build a modulo function, you will need to get user input, just like all of the other functions you made. Then, you will call the modulo function. The symbol for modulo is % You can place the modulo operator where you would normally place the division sign. Copy the following code in your Python shell as an example:

```
def modulo():
    first = int(raw_input('What is your first number?'))
    second = int(raw_input('What is your second number?'))
    print(first % second)
```

```
3  def addition():
4      first = int(raw_input('What is your first number? '))
5      second = int(raw_input('What is your second number? '))
6      print(first + second)
7
8  def subtraction():
9      first = int(raw_input('What is your first number? '))
10     second = int(raw_input('What is your second number? '))
11     print(first - second)
12
13 def multiplication():
14     first = int(raw_input('What is your first number? '))
15     second = int(raw_input('What is your second number? '))
16     print(first * second)
17
18 def division():
19     first = int(raw_input('What is your first number? '))
20     second = int(raw_input('What is your second number? '))
21     print(first / second)
22
23 def modulo():
24     first = int(raw_input('What is your first number? '))
25     second = int(raw_input('What is your second number? '))
26     print(first % second)
```

In the preceding screenshot, you can see how we added the modulo function to the other functions. If you still find modulo confusing, don't worry right away. Just know that it might come up as you are designing games, and you can check back here, as well as do an Internet, search to better understand modulo.

Running your program

To run your program, enter your command line or terminal window and type the following command:

```
python first_calc.py
```

Your program should run through addition, subtraction, multiplication, division, and modulo, and print answers to the user for each set of numbers that they enter. If there are errors when the program runs, the error messages from your computer will usually tell you that something is wrong. The error message will even tell you what line of code in your file has the problem so that it is easier to debug (find and fix errors in) your code.

A quick task for you

Q1. What kind of data does the `input()` function return?

1.   Elements
2.   Decimals
3.   Strings
4.   Integers

Q2. What does the `int()` function do?

1.   Changes data to whole numbers
2.   Changes data to a string
3.   Does nothing
4.   Changes a function into a different function

Q3. How is the `float()` function different from the `int()` function?

1.   They are not different, they do the same thing
2.   The `float()` function deals with strings only
3.   The `float()` function converts data into floating point numbers only
4.   `float()` converts words into numbers

Q4. If you make a function called `addition()` in your Python shell, how do you run that addition function to test it?

1.   Type addition in your Python shell
2.   Type def addition in your Python shell
3.   Type `addition()` in your Python shell
4.   Type `addition()` in your Python shell

Summary

Now that you have read this chapter, you hopefully have a calculator program that you can run! This program is more interactive and can do more things than your first program, so you should share this program with your family and friends to show them how you have improved your skills.

In the next chapter, we will learn about how decisions are made, and we will improve our calculator program by teaching it how to let a user choose which operation to perform as well as how many operands (numbers) to enter. We are going to get into things that are a bit more complicated, but we will go through them step by step so that you can understand each piece of what we are doing.

4
Making Decisions – Python Control Flows

Congratulations! In *Chapter 3, Calculate This!*, you wrote a calculator program. If you followed the instructions and corrected your errors, then you have a program that runs all of the mathematical functions with two numbers. While this is great for a first program, that sort of a limited calculator doesn't give a user much choice. When the user runs the calculator, the program will not end until all five functions have run or until the program ends due to an error.

What if, instead of doing the entire math, we could program our calculator to perform certain operations based on the way the users answer our questions? As programmers, we can use Python to interpret user data and change the way the program operates. In this chapter, you will learn how to use *control flows* so that our calculator program can make choices and only run the code that the user chooses.

At the end of this chapter, you will have a calculator program that can choose which mathematical operations to perform based on what the user wants to do. You will be able to customize this program on the basis of how you use the control flows.

Is it equal, not equal, or something else?

Before you learn about conditional statements, you need to realize that computers make decisions based on **comparison operators**. These help us compare two things so that the computer can make a decision about what to do next. Here is a list of operators:

Comparison Operators	
Less than	<
Less than or equal to	<=
Greater than	>
Greater than or equal to	>=
Equal to	==
Not equal to	!=

Each of these operators allows us to compare two values. The most confusing operator is the equal to operator because it uses two equals signs. The reason for this is that when we set a variable, we use one equal sign. We do not want the computer to get confused when we are comparing two values, so we use two equals signs. When we use the comparison operators with if, elif, and else, our program can be written to make better decisions.

To take a look at how these operators work in real life, open up your Python shell and type the following lines of code:

```
1 < 1
1 <= 1
1 > 1
1 >= 1
1 == 1
1 != 1
```

After each line of code, the words True or False will print. Take a look at the following screenshot for answers to how the statements evaluate using the number 1. Experiment with other numbers to take a look at what happens and to learn about the operators and what they do:

```
Python 2.7.8 (default, Jul  2 2014, 10:14:46)
[GCC 4.2.1 Compatible Apple LLVM 5.1 (clang-503.0.40)] on darwin
Type "help", "copyright", "credits" or "license" for more information.
>>> 1 < 1
False
>>> 1 <= 1
True
>>> 1 > 1
False
>>> 1 >= 1
True
>>> 1 == 1
True
>>> 1 != 1
False
>>>
```

Conditional statements – if, elif, else

There are three language constructs that are used frequently in Python to control the outcome of a program. These constructs are if, elif, and else:

- The if statement tells the program that *if the user does this, then execute this part of the program.*

- The else statement is used to catch anything that the user does and is not in the program. For example, you can use if and else together: *if the user chooses* add, *do addition, else do another action.*

> The elif stands for *else if*, which means that *if the first thing does not happen, then do the next thing in the list of possibilities until the user choice matches the possibility.*

- elif is used when you want to give the program more than two choices. You can use elif as many times as you like.

- else is a signal of the end of the possible choices to your computer program. The else means that *if none of the other things have taken place in your program, OR if the user has done something unexpected, then end this block of code.* else statements are always at the end of a block of code that begins with if.

In the next section, you can take a look at how if, elif, and else are used. Then, you will experiment with your calculator code, and add some of these statements to make your calculator more flexible.

Getting better input

In order for `if`, `elif`, and `else` to work, we will need to get better user input. For this to happen, we need to ask better questions! You will see in each example of `if`, `elif`, and `else` that we will be adding more `raw_input()` statements to get further information from the user. Then, we will put that information to work using the `if`, `elif`, and `else` statements so that our calculator program is more responsive to the user's needs.

To practice asking better questions, let's open our Python shell and practice writing the following code:

```
raw_input('add, subtract, multiply, divide, or modulo?')
```

So, we are now asking the user to choose what operation they want to execute by typing the name of the operation as the answer to the question. When our program runs, it will ask the user this question. How will our program know what to do with the answer?

if

The `if` statement tells the program to do something special if the user makes a choice. To better understand this, let's use this sample question and ask the user what operation they would like the calculator to do:

```
Python 2.7.8 (default, Jul  2 2014, 10:14:46)
[GCC 4.2.1 Compatible Apple LLVM 5.1 (clang-503.0.40)] on darwin
Type "help", "copyright", "credits" or "license" for more information.
>>>
>>> raw_input('add, subtract, multiply, divide, or modulo? ')
add, subtract, multiply, divide, or modulo? add
'add'
```

For the purposes of practicing, let's imagine that our user types *addition* as their answer. Right now, our program does not know or care that the user wants to do addition. Our program has no way to do anything with that answer! We need to use the `if` statement to tell our program what to do.

So, we will now create a special function, and we will tell the computer what to do with this new information from the user. To do this, we will use our text editor to add new code and our command prompt to run the code once we have saved the code. As a reminder, the working directory of your command prompt should be set to your project's folder.

You can refer to *Chapter 1, Welcome! Let's Get Started*, in case you've forgotten how to find your working directory.

Once you have opened your calculator program in your text editor, add this function to the program:

```
def calc_run():
    op = raw_input('add, subtract, multiply, divide, or modulo?')
    if op == 'add':
        addition()
```

Then, call your new `calc_run()` function by adding this line to the end of your program file:

```
calc_run()
```

Now, you will erase the calls you made to your addition, subtraction, multiplication, and division functions throughout the program because we do not need them all the time. We want them to happen only when the user makes the choice.

In the `calc_run()` function that we are creating now, we tell the calculator to ask a question. Once the user answers the question, the computer will check whether the answer is equal to addition. If it is, then the computer will run the addition function.

elif

The `elif` statement lets us give the user many choices, which is much more logical for a user who might want to choose from the addition, subtraction, multiplication, and division functions. Using `elif` allows us to give the user the choice between many operations. There is no limit to how many times you can write the `elif` statement.

If you wanted to create a response to 100 different kinds of information, you could write 100 `elif` statements. However, this is really tedious, so we won't do it. You can take a look at some of the changes made in the following code, which will show how you can use `elif` to give the user choices for each mathematical operation:

```
def calc_run():
    op = raw_input('add, subtract, multiply, divide, or modulo? ')
    if op == 'add':
        addition()
    elif op == 'subtract':
        subtraction()
    elif op == 'multiply':
```

```
        multiplication()
elif op == 'divide':
     division()
  elif op == 'modulo':
     modulo()
```

You will notice that we used four `elif` statements. Each `elif` matched the response that we wanted. Now, we will test our program. Hopefully, you have saved your work in your text editor. Always remember to save as often as you can!

```
3  def addition():
4      first = int(raw_input('What is your first number? '))
5      second = int(raw_input('What is your second number? '))
6      print(first + second)
7
8  def subtraction():
9      first = int(raw_input('What is your first number? '))
10     second = int(raw_input('What is your second number? '))
11     print(first - second)
12
13 def multiplication():
14     first = int(raw_input('What is your first number? '))
15     second = int(raw_input('What is your second number? '))
16     print(first * second)
17
18 def division():
19     first = int(raw_input('What is your first number? '))
20     second = int(raw_input('What is your second number? '))
21     print(first / second)
22
23 def modulo():
24     first = int(raw_input('What is your first number? '))
25     second = int(raw_input('What is your second number? '))
26     print(first % second)
27
28 def calc_run():
29     op = raw_input('add, subtract, multiply, divide, or modulo? ')
30     if op == 'add':
31         addition()
32     elif op == 'subtract':
33         subtraction()
34     elif op == 'multiply':
35         multiplication()
36     elif op == 'divide':
37         division()
38     elif op == 'modulo':
39         modulo()
40
41 calc_run()
42
```

Try running your program by following these steps:

1. Open your command prompt or terminal.

2. Navigate to your project folder.

3. Type python first_calc.py.

```
Jessicas-MacBook-Air-2:Desktop jessicanickel$ python first_calc.py
add, subtract, multiply, divide, or modulo? add
What is your first number? 4
What is your second number? 32
36
```

else

else is a way to manage all the other things that a user might do that we cannot predict. When the user enters something to trigger else, we can return a message to them, or we can even end the program. Your program does not *NEED* to use an else statement; however, it is nice to make the choices that you want for your users, and make them as clear as possible. In the following example, we will print a message to the user if they do *NOT* choose add, subtract, multiply, divide, or modulo:

```python
def calc_run():
    op = raw_input('add, subtract, multiply, divide, or modulo? ')
    if op == 'add':
        addition()
    elif op == 'subtract':
        subtraction()
    elif op == 'multiply':
        multiplication()
    elif op == 'divide':
        division()
    elif op == 'modulo':
        modulo()
    else:
        print('Thank you. Goodbye')
```

```python
32 def calc_run():
33     op = raw_input('add, subtract, multiply, divide, or modulo? ')
34     if op == 'add':
35         addition()
36     elif op == 'subtract':
37         subtraction()
38     elif op == 'multiply':
39         multiplication()
40     elif op == 'divide':
41         division()
42     elif op == 'modulo':
43         modulo()
44     else:
45         print('Thank you. Goodbye')
46
```

Now, when you run the code, if you type an answer that is not addition, subtraction, multiplication, or division, your program should print Thank you. Goodbye. Test your program to check whether your else statement works!

```
Jessicas-MacBook-Air-2:~ jessicanickel$ cd Desktop
Jessicas-MacBook-Air-2:Desktop jessicanickel$ python first_calc.py
add, subtract, multiply, divide, or modulo? none of these
Thank you. Goodbye
Jessicas-MacBook-Air-2:Desktop jessicanickel$ █
```

Loops

Loops are a kind of control flow, but they rerun the same block of code over and over again until something else tells the loop to stop repeating itself. This is a bit different from conditional statements since these only run the block of code once. The two kinds of loop are while and for. Both types of loop are really useful.

while

while is one kind of loop. When we make a while loop, the program repeats itself until a given block of code happens. When programming a while loop, we need to create some rules, or our program will run forever.

For example, we can make this rule: when the calculator is on, perform the following steps:

1. Run the calculator.
2. Prompt the user to keep calculating.
3. When the user hits the else statement, turn the calculator off.

Let's go through each of the code changes step by step; you will need these changes in order to make the while loop work.

Global variables and the quit() function

We will create a global variable to use in our quit() function. Using the variable in this way will allow us to let the quit () function act like an off switch, thus stopping our calc_run() function from running. In the next section, we will write our global variable, and then we will create our quit() function.

First, we will make a global variable called `calc_on`. This is one way for us to make an `on` button for our computer calculator. This global variable should be typed at the top of the code file with the *NO* indentation:

```
calc_on = 1
```

Global variables can be used in any function we want throughout the program. If you want to use a global variable in a function, you can type `global` next to the name of the variable inside of the function. You will be shown an example of this later on.

Now that we have an *on button* global variable that can be used anywhere in our code, we will create the pieces needed for our `while` loop. We need to add a way for our program to keep repeating itself so that the user can keep doing calculations without restarting the program for each calculation. Also, we need to add a way for the user to quit the program. We are going to work backward and make the `quit()` function first:

```python
def quit():
  global calc_on
  calc_on = 0
```

We just wrote the code for our `quit()` function. The first line uses our `calc_on` global variable. The second line changes the value of `calc_on` to `0`. By changing the value from `1` to `0`, we are telling the program to turn the calculator off and stop running the code.

Using the quit() function

In our code, we are going to change our `else` statement so that it runs the `quit()` function instead of printing a message. Take a look at this code sample to understand the changes we make to else:

```python
def calc_run():
    op = raw_input('add, subtract, multiply, divide, or modulo? ')
  if op == 'add':
      addition()
  elif op == 'subtract':
      subtraction()
  elif op == 'multiply':
      multiplication()
  elif op == 'divide':
      division()
```

```
  elif op == 'modulo':
      modulo()
  else:
      quit()
```

Now that we have made the on button, `calc_on`, the `off` button, and `quit()`, we can add the `quit` choice to our program. In the line of code where we get information from the user, we will add the word `quit` as a choice:

```
op = raw_input('add, subtract, multiply, divide, modulo, quit?')
```

Using the while loop to control the program

Quitting is one choice that the user can make by simply typing `quit`. However, we want to allow the user to keep the program running if they wish to. To do this, we will use a `while` loop. At the bottom of the code, we will simply write this:

```
while calc_on == 1:
    calc_run()
```

The `while` loop is says that *while the on button is on, run the* `calc_run()` *function. If someone does something to change* `calc_on` *to a value that is not* 1, *then stop running the* `calc_run()` *program.*

Hopefully, you noticed that our `quit()` function changes the value of `calc_on` to 0, which means that our program stops running. `while` loops are very useful for running run parts of a program, and they can use simple variables to start or stop the loops, which is similar to what we did with this calculator:

```
27
28 def quit():
29     global calc_on
30     calc_on = 0
31
32 def calc_run():
33     op = raw_input('add, subtract, multiply, divide, or modulo? ')
34     if op == 'add':
35         addition()
36     elif op == 'subtract':
37         subtraction()
38     elif op == 'multiply':
39         multiplication()
40     elif op == 'divide':
41         division()
42     elif op == 'modulo':
43         modulo()
44     else:
45         quit()
46
47 while calc_on == 1:
48     calc_run()
```

for

The for loop is another kind of loop. We will use the for loop to make a bonus function for our calculator. The biggest difference between for and while is that the for loop is used when a programmer knows exactly how many times they need the loop to repeat. In the while loop, we do not know when the user will be done with the calculator. The user might want to make one calculation or they might want to make 10, and a while loop is flexible. A for loop is more rigid.

Why not just use while all the time, then? Well, there are times when we know just what it will take to get a job done, and we do not want the program to keep going any more after the job is done. The for loop is perfect for saying how many times to repeat a loop. For example, let's say that you have a list of numbers, and you want to print all the numbers in the list. Let's say that you want to print the numbers 1 through 10. If you had to write them out individually, it would look like this:

```
print(1)
print(2)
print(3)
print(4)
print(5)
print(6)
print(7)
print(8)
print(9)
print(10)
```

This is a lot of lines of code, and they are all doing the same thing! What a waste of space, and what a waste of time to type this all out. Instead of typing the preceding code, type the code in the following `for` loop:

```
for n in range(1, 11):
    print(n)
```

```
>>>
>>>
>>>
>>>
>>>
>>>
>>>
>>>
>>>
>>>
>>> for n in range(1, 11):
...     print(n)
...
1
2
3
4
5
6
7
8
9
10
>>>
```

First, you see that we typed n in `range(1, 11)`. This means *every number between* 1 *and* 11, *not including* 11.

You will also notice that we called a function named `range()`, which is a built-in Python function that allows us to specify a range of numbers instead of writing them all out. The `range()` function does *NOT* include the last number, so you can see that the second number is 11, instead of 10.

You can experiment with these numbers in the range by expanding it to `range (1, 1000)`. What happens now? This is a basic `for` loop, but we will find that using this `for` loop is very helpful when we want to repeat code for lists of numbers, letters, words, or objects.

Bonus – count_to_ten() function

To make our calculator a little more interesting, let's create a `count` function that will print the numbers from `1` to `10`. We can then add this function to our list of choices. First, think about how we used the preceding `for` loop. Then, copy the `count_to_ten()` function between the `modulo()` function and the `quit()` function into your `first_calc.py` program:

```
def count_to_ten()
    for number in range(1, 11):
            print(number)
```

Add the choice `ten` to your `op` variable, like this:

```
        op = raw_input('add, subtract, multiply, divide, modulo, ten, or
quit?')
```

Finally, add `elif` for `ten` to your control flow of `if`/`elif`/`else`:

```
elif op == 'ten':
    count_to_ten()
```

This will print out the choice for your users, and then, when they type `ten`, the calculator will print out all of the numbers from 1 to 10. This screenshot shows how the code works:

```
Jessicas-MacBook-Air-2:Desktop jessicanickel$ python first_calc.py
add, subtract, multiply, divide, modulo, ten, or quit? ten
1
2
3
4
5
6
7
8
9
10
add, subtract, multiply, divide, modulo, ten, or quit? quit
Jessicas-MacBook-Air-2:Desktop jessicanickel$ 
```

A quick task for you

In this chapter, you learned a lot about how to write programs that can make decisions. Here are some questions to answer:

Q1. How many times can the `elif` statement appear in the `if/elif/else` flow?

1. Only once
2. Twice
3. As many times as it is needed
4. Ten

Q2. Which statement starts a conditional block of code that is used to make decisions?

1. else
2. if
3. elif
4. while

Q3. Which statement is only used at the end of a conditional block of code?

1. else
2. if
3. elif
4. while

Q4. What is a global variable?

1. A variable that is only used in one function
2. A variable that can be shared with many functions
3. A variable that uses global before its name if it is inside a function
4. Both 2 and 3

Q5. What is a `while` loop?

1. A loop that runs code only once
2. A loop that runs code a set number of times
3. A loop that repeats code until something different happens, and then it stops
4. A loop that does nothing

Summary

In this chapter, you learned many new concepts. You learned about comparison operators, the symbols that allow us to compare two items. You also learned about `if`, `elif`, and `else`, which are three conditional words that let us tell our program how to make different decisions based on the information that a user enters. You learned about the `for` and `while` loops; both are very important in making programs that give feedback. You also learned a bit about how to use global variables, which can be shared with all the functions in a code file.

Hopefully, you are keeping up with everything we've talked about so far! It may feel a little overwhelming, but we will continue to review the concepts we learned in this chapter by building some new projects in the next chapter.

5

Loops and Logic

In the previous chapter, you learned how to use logic, such as `if`, `elif`, and `else`, to help design programs that could respond to user input in many ways. Also, you learned how to use the `while` and `for` loops. In this chapter, we will build our first mini game, called **Higher** or **Lower**. The game is a number guessing game, and we will use it to combine logic and loops to make a game that responds to many user requests.

 Remember to save your work frequently so that you can make corrections to your code!

Higher or Lower

Higher or Lower is a numbers guessing game. In this game, the computer chooses a random number, and the user tries to guess what number the computer has chosen. There are many different ways to build this game, and many versions of this game have been built by different people.

Our version of the game will have two levels:

- An easy level
- A hard level

The computer will first choose a random, secret number between 1 and 100. In the easy level, the user will get unlimited chances to guess the correct number. In the hard level, the user will only get three chances to guess the correct number, and then they will lose the game.

This game can be coded in different ways and still work well—this is one of the most awesome things about writing code. However, we will focus on writing code that uses a `while` loop for the easy version and a `for` loop for the hard version. This will let us practice our loops and build a game that has different levels of challenge.

To be successful in this chapter, follow each section step by step, and make sure that you understand what is happening before moving on to the next section. Test your code by running your program when you are instructed in the text so that you learn how things work. At the end of this chapter, you will have your first fully functioning game!

Game file set up

When you start to think about a small game such as Higher or Lower, you can write some of your code like an outline for a book, that is, you can use comments to place all of the logic in your code, even if you are not certain how exactly the code works. In our file, we need to set up code for the easy version and hard version, a function to start the game, and a function to end the game.

To start planning the game, you need to keep your coding tools ready:

- Open up your Notepad++ (Windows) or jEdit (Mac/Linux) to write the code
- Open up your command prompt (Windows) or terminal (Mac/Linux), and navigate to your project folder
- Open up your Python shell so that you can test code while you are working

In your text editor, make a new file, and save it with the name `higher_lower.py`.

Then, write comments for the easy version. Single line comments in the Python code start with a pound sign or hashtag:

```
# this is a comment
```

Write the following comments in your file, leaving some spaces between each comment line, and then save your work:

```
# imported libraries go here


# global variables go here


# function for easy version
```

```
# function for hard version


# function to start game


# function to stop game


# function calls go here
```

Take a look at the following screenshot of what this will look like in your text editor:

```
1 # imported libraries go here
2
3 # global variables go here
4
5 # function for easy version
6
7 # function for hard version
8
9 # function to start game
10
11 # function to stop game
12
13 # function calls go here
```

Importing libraries

For this Higher or Lower game, we will import the random library. This library has functions that we will use to choose a random number to start each game. Starting with a random number each time means that the game experience will be new for the player because they need to guess a different number each time they play. To import a Python library, we use the import statement and the name of the library. In your code file, replace # imported libraries go here and comment with the following:

```
import random
```

Importing the random library allows us access to many functions that create random numbers and strings in different ways. There are even ways to create secure strings and numbers that would work well if you have to write a password-making program!

Setting and initializing global variables

Now that we have imported the library that we need, we will set our global variables. As a reminder, a global variable is a variable that can be used anywhere throughout the code file. Global variables are helpful, as we saw with our calculator, because we can use them to define the status or state of a program and change the state of the program in different functions.

For example, in our calculator, we had a global variable called `calc_on`. In this Higher or Lower game, we will have a few global variables that we set. Replace `# global variables go here` and comment with these lines:

```
game_on = None
guesses = None


secret = None
```

The `game_on` variable keeps running the program. The `guesses` variable states how many guesses users will get. The `secret` variable is the number that the computer chooses at `random`, and it changes every time the game restarts.

These global variables are different than the ones we used for the previous chapter, though. These global variables are set to equal `None`. Why? Well, setting the global variables equal to none simply allows them to be reset from `None` or zero each time that they are called in the program. You will take a look at the places where we call global variables into a function, and then reset the value.

What is a Boolean?

We are going to be using the words **True** and **False** to help run our game programs in both the easy and difficult versions of the game. In computer programming, in most languages, these words have a special name: **Boolean**. What is a Boolean?

A Boolean can only have two values: true or false. Booleans are helpful when there are only these two possibilities for a variable. For example, a game can be on or off. We have a global variable called `game_on`. If this variable is set to `True`, it means that our game is running. If it is set to `False`, it means that our game has stopped.

In *Chapter 4*, *Making Decisions – Python Control Flows*, you learned about how the comparison of two statements can print out the `True` or `False` statements. In this chapter, we are going to use the `True` and `False` conditions to control whether our program is running or not.

Building the easy version

Now that we have set up our global variables and imported our library, we can work on the logic needed to make the easy version of our game. This block of code tells the computer what to do if the user decides to play the easy version of the game.

First, we need to name and define the function:

```
def difficulty_level_easy():
```

It is good to name your function so that you remember what it does. After naming the function, the first thing we need is the information from our global variables. We will set the global variables in this function for the secret variable. We bring in these variables as the first two lines in the function, and we have to type `global` in front of the names of the variable:

```
def difficulty_level_easy():
   global secret
   secret = int(random.randrange(0,100))
```

We have reset the `secret` global variable from `None` to an integer between `0` and `99` using `int (random.randrange(0,100))`. This means that when the game starts, a number between `0` and `99` will be selected as the secret number that the user must guess. Now, we need to create what people call the *win condition*. In other words, we need to program what winning and losing means. Let's think this through.

 Can you talk through what it means to win the game and lose it? Can you draw a diagram? Try it yourself before copying the code!

Hopefully, you attempted to figure out how the game will work before you looked at this section of the book. Solving difficult problems is a key part of building games, and problem solving is a skill that is developed with practice. So, we will now write the code that decides whether the player wins or loses.

The win condition in the easy version of the game is that the user guesses the correct number in as many guesses as they need. To keep our game running, we are going to use a `while` loop, which we learned about in *Chapter 4, Making Decisions – Python Control Flows*. `while` loops are helpful when we are running a loop but we do not know how many times we need the loop to run. Our `while` loop will run as long as `game_on = True`. For the easy game, we are going to assume that `game_on` is `True`. We will write the function for `game_on` later:

```
def difficulty_level_easy():
   secret = float(random.randrange(0,100))
   while game_on:
```

We have written the code to set a number and run the game. Now, we need to put some commands into the `while` loop so that it knows what to do. The first thing that we want the user to do is make a guess at the number, so we need to use the `raw_input()` function to get information from the user. We will add this input line to our function:

```
def difficulty_level_easy():
    secret = float(random.randrange(0,100))
    while game_on:
        guess = int(input('Guess a number. '))
```

Look at the last line of code that we added. The variable `guess` is set equal to the user's input. We are using `int()` to turn the user input from a string into a number because the game is generating random numbers, *NOT* random strings. We want to compare numbers to numbers. In fact, we *HAVE* to compare numbers to numbers. The program will not work if you do not add `int()` around the `raw_input()` function. Make sure you understand what the last line of code means before moving forward.

Also, you may notice that there is an extra space after the period in the raw input statement: `guess = int(input('Guess a number. '))`. Adding a space after the period and before the end of the string will tell the computer to print an extra space so that it will be easier for the user to read their code. See the following screenshots that show the difference the space makes.

Here is the code with no extra space:

```
Jessicas-MacBook-Air-2:Chapter5 jessicanickel$ python higher_lower.py
Welcome. Type easy, hard, or quit. easy
Guess a number.3
```

Notice that the output is easier to read when we add an extra space after the period:

```
Jessicas-MacBook-Air-2:Chapter5 jessicanickel$ python higher_lower.py
Welcome. Type easy, hard, or quit. easy
Guess a number. 2
```

Compare numbers

Our next lines of code involve decision making. We have to tell the computer what to do if the user gets the number too high or too low. We also have to tell the computer what to do when the user wins. To tell the computer what to do, we can perform three steps:

1. Compare the user guess to the secret computer number.

2. Output instructions to the user based on whether they guessed too high, too low, or just right.

3. To compare numbers, we will use the comparison operators that we learned about in *Chapter 4, Making Decisions – Python Control Flows*. We will need three operators: greater than (>), less than (<), and equal to (==).

Because there are three possible choices, we need to use if, elif, and else to tell the computer what possible things can happen.

First, let's explain the logic using words. Then, we can convert this into code. It is good to learn to think through these problems before you start coding. This helps you know what outcome to expect:

*   if the user's number is less than the secret computer number, print Your guess is too low

*   Or else (elif), if the user's number is higher than the secret computer number, print Your guess is too high

*   Or else, if the user's number is the same as the secret computer number, then we print You win!

 Can you draw, write, or imagine how this code will work before looking at the next section?

Now that you have thought about the logic of the next section, here is what the code looks like once it is added to the function:

```
def difficulty_level_easy():
    global secret
    global gameOn
    while gameOn == 'true':
        guess = float(input('Guess a number. '))
        if guess > secret:
            print('your guess is too high. Try again.')
        elif guess < secret:
            print('your guess is too low. Try again.')
        elif guess == secret:
            print('You win!')
            play_again()
```

We have seven new lines of code that we are adding for each possibility that the user can enter:

- *If the user guess is too high,* the user must enter another number, and the while loop returns to run the code again

- *If the user guess is too low,* then the user must enter another number, and the while loop returns to run the code again

 Since this is the easy version, the while loop will run until the user finally guesses the correct number no matter how many incorrect guesses the user makes.

- *When the user guess is the same as the computer number,* then the program prints You win! and calls a function called play_again()

play_again()

There is a function called play_again() that we added to the end of the difficulty_level_easy() function. We are calling one function inside of another, which we have done earlier. However, we have to make this play_again() function because it doesn't exist yet.

The play_again() function will ask the users whether they want to play the game again and then make a decision about running the program. When the while loop finally runs the play_again() function, it ends the loop of code in the difficulty_level_easy() function and goes on to run its own code. In the next section of the chapter, we will create the functions needed to start, stop, and play again:

```
2  import random
3
4  game_on = None
5
6  guesses = None
7
8  secret = None
9
10
11 def difficulty_level_easy():
12     global secret
13     secret = int(random.randrange(0,100))
14     while game_on:
15         guess = int(raw_input('Guess a number .'))
16         if guess > secret:
17             print('your guess is too high. Try again.')
18         elif guess < secret:
19             print('your guess is too low. Try again.')
20         elif guess == secret:
21             print('You win!')
22             play_again()
```

Start, stop, play again

So, if you are here, it is because you built the easy version of the game, and you want to test it out, play it, and see whether it actually works. If you try running the code right now, one of two things will happen: if it is perfect, then nothing will happen. If you have a problem in your code, you will get an error message. Either way, you cannot run the program with the code as it is right now because your program has no way to start itself!

Let's build some helper functions that will start our code and allow us to play the game again. We will write two helper functions: `start_game()` and `play_again()`. We can end the loop and change the `game_on` Boolean to `False` at the end of the `start_game()` and `play_again()` functions.

start_game()

In your `higher_lower.py` file, where you wrote the `# function to start game` comment, write this instead:

```
def start_game():
```

We have defined the function that will start our game. The next step is to invoke (use) our `game_on` global variable, and then set the variable to `True`. This tells the function that the game is in the on state:

```
def start_game():
    global  game_on
    game_on = True
```

Once we tell the computer to start, we need the user to tell the computer what they want to do. Using the `raw_input()` function, we are ready to get information from our player. We will make a variable called `level`. That variable will take input from the user. We will give the user three choices: easy, hard, or quit. Add the following lines of code in your file, and make sure to save your work:

```
def start_game():

    global game_on
    game_on = True     level = input('Welcome. Type easy, hard, or quit
.')
```

Now that we have information from the user stored in the `level` variable, we can use it to inform the comparison operators, and we can use the `if`/`elif` logic to make a decision about what to do in our program.

Here are some examples:

- If the user types `easy`, then the computer will run the `difficulty_level_easy()` function

- Or else (`elif`), if the user types `hard`, then the computer will run the hard version of the game (`difficulty_level_hard()` function)

- Or else (`elif`), if the user decides to quit, then we will stop the program from running by changing the Boolean of `game_on` to equal `False`

Adding logic for the computer to start the correct game based on the user choice will take six new lines of code:

```
def start_game():
    global game_on
    level = input('Welcome. Type easy, hard, or quit. ')
    if level == 'easy':
        difficulty_level_easy()
    elif level == 'hard':
        difficulty_level_hard()
    elif level == 'quit':
        game_on = False
```

An important thing to notice about the last line of code is that we changed the `game_on` global variable to `False`, causing the program to end. Also, notice how our `start_game()` function calls the other functions inside of it. So, the `difficulty_level_easy()` function that we made starts to run when someone types easy.

play_again()

The last helper function is the `play_again()` function. This function, which we used at the end of the `difficulty_level_easy()` function, allows the user to make a choice of whether to play again or not. By now, you are probably starting to see a pattern with regard to what we do with information from `raw_input` in order to help the computer make choices. We use `if`, `elif`, and `else` to compare the user's choice to a set of choices that we have programmed. Then, we program the result of the choice to be what we want.

For the `play_again()` function, the user will be asked whether they would like to play again. We will prompt the user to type Yes or No:

```
def play_again():
    global game_on
      game_on = True
        play = input('Play again? Yes or No. ')
```

With our program, we are only accepting two user choices so that we can use `if` and `else` to explain what should happen. If the user types Yes, then the `start_game()` function will run and our program will continue. If the user types No, then the `game_on` variable will be set to `False` and the program will stop. So, we will add four more lines of code:

```
def play_again():
    global gameOn
    play = input('Play again? Yes or No.')
    if play == 'Yes':
        start_game()
  else:
        gameOn = 'false'
```

Play testing

Once you have made the `play_again()` function, you only need to add one more line of code to test the easy version of your game! The last line of your code file will be calling the `start_game()` function. Add this code to the bottom of your game file:

```
start_game()
```

Once the `start_game()` line is added, you will be able to test the easy version of your game. Now is a good point to stop, save, and test. Play the game many times to make sure you fully understand how it works. Ask others to play it as well.

You might decide to change some of the input questions to add humor to make them funny or get different results. It is up to you to test your code changes and to make sure they work!

```
41
42  def start_game():
43      global game_on
44      game_on = True
45      level = raw_input('Welcome. Type easy, hard, or quit. ')
46      if level == 'easy':
47          difficulty_level_easy()
48      elif level == 'hard':
49          difficulty_level_hard()
50      elif level == 'quit':
51          game_on = False
52          print('Thanks for playing')
53
54
55  def play_again():
56      global game_on
57      game_on = True
58      play = raw_input('Play again? Yes or No. ')
59      if play == 'Yes':
60          start_game()
61      else:
62          game_on = False
63          print ('Thanks for playing.')
64
65  start_game()
```

 Save your work and test your code! Go to your terminal and navigate to your project folder.

When you type the following code line, your code should begin to run inside of your command prompt or terminal. To test the code, make sure you answer easy so that you can run the version of the code that you have made:

```
python higher_lower.py
```

```
Jessicas-MacBook-Air-2:~ jessicanickel$ cd Desktop
Jessicas-MacBook-Air-2:Desktop jessicanickel$ python3.5 higher_lower.py
Welcome. Type easy, hard, or quit. easy
Guess a number. 33
your guess is too low. Try again.
Guess a number. 66
your guess is too high. Try again.
Guess a number. 35
your guess is too low. Try again.
Guess a number. 45
your guess is too low. Try again.
Guess a number. 56
your guess is too low. Try again.
Guess a number. 57
your guess is too low. Try again.
Guess a number. 60
your guess is too high. Try again.
Guess a number. 59
You win!
Play again? Yes or No.No
Jessicas-MacBook-Air-2:Desktop jessicanickel$
```

Building the hard version

The hard version of the game uses exactly the same *win conditions* as the easy version of the game. There is only one difference.

The hard version only allows the player to make three guesses before it resets the game! Therefore, we can use a `for` loop to define that we only want the program to run three times if the player does not guess the correct number.

First, we will define the function for the hard version of the game:

```
def difficulty_level_hard():
```

Next, we will add our global variables. In the hard version of the game, we need to use the global variable `guesses`, which we will set to three for this program:

```
def difficulty_level_hard():

    global guesses
    guesses = 3
```

Now, we need to create the logic. Here, we will use a `for` loop so that our loop only runs the number of times that we wish it to run. So, we will add a line of code that says `i in range (guesses)`, which means that for every number in the range of numbers of guesses, run our code.

First, let's add this line of code, and then we will go over each part:

```
def difficulty_level_hard():


    global guesses
    guesses = 3
    for i in range(guesses):
```

The letter `i` is used to mean one single number. The word `range` is used to tell the computer to go over the total number of `guesses`, which we set to `3`.

Next, we will write the code to get user input, compare the user number to the secret computer number, and use the `if`/`elif` logic to print output messages to the user and run the loop again.

Before you copy the code of the `for` loop into your program, figure out if you can write, draw, or explain how the `for` loop will work differently than the `while` loop did. If you can understand the differences, you will learn a lot more about how your `for` loop works.

Comparing numbers – the hard version

What exactly is the logic when using a `for` loop instead of a `while` loop? As we noted earlier, the `for` loop is more defined to run a specific number of times. So, with our for `i in range(guesses)`, we are really saying this:

- For the first guess, do this thing
- For the second guess, do this thing
- For the third guess, if the player is still incorrect, stop the `for` loop, print the message, and run the `play_again()` function

Now that you have a better concept of the logic, let's add these lines of code to the `for` loop in our `difficulty_level_hard()` function:

```
def difficulty_level_hard():
    global random
    global guesses
    for i in range(guesses):
        guess = float(input('Guess a number. '))
        if i == 2:
            print('Game over. Too many guesses.')
            play_again()
        elif guess > secret:
            print('your guess is too high. Try again.')
        elif guess < secret:
            print('your guess is too low. Try again.')
        elif guess == secret:
            print('You win!')
            play_again()
```

As you can see, in the first line of code beneath the `for` loop, we use a `raw_input()` function that we assign to the variable `guess` to get information from the user. Then, we make *win conditions* for the hard version of the game. In this case, if `i` (the number of `guesses`) is equal to 2, then the game restarts. This is because the range function we are using starts counting from `zero`, so the three computer numbers are 0, 1, and 2. The first two lines of our `for` loop use a comparison operator (`==`) to check whether the user has had too many guesses. If the user *HAS* tried too many times, then the loop ends and the `Game over. Too many guesses` message is printed.

We have decided what happens if the user has too many guesses in the `for` loop. Now, we will define what happens if a player is too high or too low in terms of their guess. We use the same comparison operators of greater than (`>`), less than (`<`), and equal to (`==`) that we used in the easy version, and we print a message if the user is too high or too low.

Notice that we call the play_again() function twice. We offer the user the chance to play_again() if they lose by guessing too many times or when they win. Losing and winning are both times when the for loop will stop running, so we need to make sure we have added the play_again() function after both of these conditions:

```
Jessicas-MacBook-Air-2:Chapter5 jessicanickel$ python higher_lower.py
Welcome. Type easy, hard, or quit. hard
Guess a number. 5
your guess is too low. Try again.
Guess a number. 9
your guess is too low. Try again.
Guess a number. 87
Game over. Too many guesses.
Play again? Yes or No. No
Thanks for playing.
Jessicas-MacBook-Air-2:Chapter5 jessicanickel$ █
```

Play test the whole program!

Now you get to see exactly how you did! Go to your terminal and run your program again by typing the following command:

```
python higher_lower.py
```

First, make sure that the program works. If you get errors right away, double-check your code to make sure it does not have any problems, such as:

- spacing or indents

- typos

- syntax (punctuation)

These are some common problems that people have with their programs. Usually, you will get an error message called Trace or stacktrace that will tell you what line in your code is causing the problem. Here is an example of what happens when the user types the word three instead of the number 3:

```
Jessicas-MacBook-Air-2:Chapter5 jessicanickel$ python higher_lower.py
Welcome. Type easy, hard, or quit. easy
Guess a number. three
Traceback (most recent call last):
  File "higher_lower.py", line 67, in <module>
    start_game()
  File "higher_lower.py", line 49, in start_game
    difficulty_level_easy()
  File "higher_lower.py", line 15, in difficulty_level_easy
    guess = int(raw_input('Guess a number. '))
ValueError: invalid literal for int() with base 10: 'three'
```

There are some things called *test cases* that you will want to try before letting other people play your game. Good programmers need to think about how their program works, and they also need to think about the things a user can do that might break the program. The following are some tests you can run. Some might break your program:

- Does your game work in both the easy *AND* the hard version?
- What happens if you type `quit`?
- What happens if you enter a number higher than 99?
- What happens when you type the word `three` instead of the number `3`?
- Can you force the program to print errors (there are ways to make your program have errors, so be creative)? If so, notice your error messages, and think about how to prevent errors.

There are some errors that you might not understand, and that is okay. You can always perform an Internet search to look up the error message and check what other people have learned about it.

Once you have tested the game and feel ready to share it, ask others to play it and watch as they interact with your game. Ask yourself some questions while you watch your user play:

- What was easy for the user to understand?
- What was hard for the user to understand?
- What errors did the user make?
- How could I change the game code to make the game better?

As a programmer, you will learn how to be a creative problem solver. If you see something in this program that you want to rewrite, you should try it! Keep a backup copy of your working code, and then start to experiment with some different options. Some examples you can use are as follows:

- Make the range of the hard program larger so that it is more difficult for the user to guess correctly (`0, 1000`)
- Add your own personal touch to each message
- Add a variable to take the username and print it

Each of the preceding examples are ways in which you can challenge yourself and take the program further! Check your program against the following screenshot, and figure out whether you can answer some quick questions about what you learned in this chapter:

```
24
25 def difficulty_level_hard():
26     global guesses
27     global secret
28     guesses = 3
29     secret = int(random.randrange(0,100))
30     for i in range(guesses):
31         guess = int(raw_input('Guess a number. '))
32         if i == 2:
33             print('Game over. Too many guesses.')
34             play_again()
35         elif guess > secret:
36             print('your guess is too high. Try again.')
37         elif guess < secret:
38             print('your guess is too low. Try again.')
39         elif guess == secret:
40             print('You win!')
41             play_again()
42
43
44 def start_game():
45     global game_on
46     game_on = True
47     level = raw_input('Welcome. Type easy, hard, or quit. ')
48     if level == 'easy':
49         difficulty_level_easy()
50     elif level == 'hard':
51         difficulty_level_hard()
52     elif level == 'quit':
53         game_on = False
54         print('Thanks for playing')
55
56
57 def play_again():
58     global game_on
59     game_on = True
60     play = raw_input('Play again? Yes or No. ')
61     if play == 'Yes':
62         start_game()
63     else:
64         game_on = False
65         print ('Thanks for playing.')
66
67 start_game()
```

A quick task for you

Q1. What is a Boolean?

1. A statement that is either `True` or `False`

2. A statement with many possible outcomes

3. Used as a variable name

4. Used as a place

Q2. Why are global variables helpful?

1. They are limited to what they can do
2. They can be used in any function in the file where they are set
3. They can be changed inside the function
4. Choice 2 and 3

Q3. `for` loops are similar to `while` loops. How is a `for` loop different from a `while` loop?

1. `for` loops are used to loop a specified number of times
2. `for` loops are used only for text
3. `for` loops are used only for numbers
4. `for` loops can only work with dictionaries

Q4. What would be a good time to use a `while` loop in a game?

1. To run a game a specified number of times
2. To run a game forever
3. To keep a game going while a certain condition is true
4. To end the game

Q5. What symbol is used to write comments in the code that are not a part of the code?

1. ?
2. *
3. ()
4. #

Summary

In this chapter, we learned how to build a game using loops and logic. The game, Higher or Lower, has an easy version and a difficult version. Input from the player is used by the game to make decisions about what code will run next.

In the next chapter, we will learn about how to work with some data, including how to store and retrieve information. These skills will help us to learn how to do things such as ask for player names, include player names in our games, and store scores in the program. All of these skills are important to build a complete and interesting game experience.

6
Working with Data – Lists and Dictionaries

In the previous chapter, you learned how to write loops using detailed logic in order to help you help your program to make decisions. So far, though, you have not yet learned what to do with data. We have not created nor stored data. Yet, we know that video games store data! Video games sometimes store the names of players as well as the highest score that a player has achieved. How does one computer program remember all of this information? In this chapter, you will learn about some ways that Python can store and retrieve data, such as lists and dictionaries.

For the exercises and code in this chapter, your Python shell will be the best tool to use so that you can type your lists and dictionaries and then check the outcome of your coding. Otherwise, once your prompt is available, you can type lists and dictionaries, your shell will remember the information that you enter, and then you can test how to retrieve, add, and remove information.

 If you shut down your Python shell at any time during this chapter, all of your work will be lost. The Python shell does not remember information between sessions, so lists and dictionaries will not be saved.

Lists

Lists have many different uses when coding, and many different operations can be performed on lists, thanks to Python. In this chapter, you will only learn about some of the many uses of lists.

If you wish to learn more about lists, the Python documentation is very detailed and can be found at https://docs.python.org/3/ tutorial/datastructures.html?highlight=lists#more-on- lists.

First, some facts about Python lists: Python lists are *mutable*. This means that the data in a list can be changed around. Items can be added or removed using functions that act directly on the list. Also, the items in a list can be mixed together. Numbers, floats, and strings can all go together in the same list.

Parts of a list

Lists, like other kinds of data, are assigned to a variable. Then, the list items are placed in [ ]:

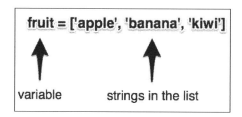

In your Python shell, type the following three lists, one on each line:

```
fruit = ['apple', 'banana', 'kiwi', 'dragonfruit']
years = [2012,   2013,   2014,   2015]
students_in_class = [30,   22,   28,   33]
```

```
Last login: Tue Dec  8 21:40:12 on ttys000
Jessicas-MacBook-Air-2:~ jessicanickel$ python3.5
Python 3.5.0 (v3.5.0:374f501f4567, Sep 12 2015, 11:00:19)
[GCC 4.2.1 (Apple Inc. build 5666) (dot 3)] on darwin
Type "help", "copyright", "credits" or "license" for more information.
>>>
>>>
>>> fruit = ['apple', 'banana', 'kiwi', 'dragonfruit']
>>> years = [2012, 2013, 2014, 2015]
>>> students_in_class = [30, 22, 28, 33]
>>>
>>>
```

Each of the lists you have typed has a particular kind of data inside it. The `fruit` list contains strings, the `years` list contains integers, and the `students_in_class` list also contains integers. However, one feature of lists is that they can mix up datatypes within the same list. For example, I have made this list that combines strings and integers:

```
computer_class = ['Cynthia', 78, 42, 'Raj', 98, 24, 35, 'Kadeem',
'Rachel']
```

Working with a list

Now that we have made the lists, we can work with the contents of the list in many ways. In fact, once you create a list, the computer remembers the order of the list, and the order stays constant until it is changed purposefully. The easiest way for us to check whether the order of lists is maintained is to run tests on the `fruit`, `years`, `students_in_class`, and `computer_class` lists that we have already made.

The first item of a Python list is always counted as **0 (zero)**. So, for our first test, let's check whether asking for item `0` actually gives us the first item we entered in the list. Using our `fruit` list, we will type the name of the list inside a `print` statement, and then add square brackets `[]` with the number `0`:

```
print(fruit[0])
```

Your output should be `apple` since apple is the first fruit in the list we created earlier:

```
Last login: Tue Dec  8 21:40:12 on ttys000
Jessicas-MacBook-Air-2:~ jessicanickel$ python3.5
Python 3.5.0 (v3.5.0:374f501f4567, Sep 12 2015, 11:00:19)
[GCC 4.2.1 (Apple Inc. build 5666) (dot 3)] on darwin
Type "help", "copyright", "credits" or "license" for more information.
>>>
>>>
>>> fruit = ['apple', 'banana', 'kiwi', 'dragonfruit']
>>> years = [2012, 2013, 2014, 2015]
>>> students_in_class = [30, 22, 28, 33]
>>>
>>> print(fruit[0])
apple
>>>
```

Now, we have evidence that counting in Python does start with 0 and also that our list is written correctly. Next, we can try to print the fourth item in the `fruit` list. You will notice that we are entering 3 in our `print` command. This is because the first item started at 0. Type this code into your Python shell:

```
print(fruit[3])
```

What is your outcome? Did you expect `dragonfruit` to be the answer? If so, good, you are learning to count items in lists. If not, remember that the first item in a list is item 0. With practice, you will become better at counting items in short Python lists:

```
Last login: Tue Dec  8 21:40:12 on ttys000
Jessicas-MacBook-Air-2:~ jessicanickel$ python3.5
Python 3.5.0 (v3.5.0:374f501f4567, Sep 12 2015, 11:00:19)
[GCC 4.2.1 (Apple Inc. build 5666) (dot 3)] on darwin
Type "help", "copyright", "credits" or "license" for more information.
>>>
>>>
>>> fruit = ['apple', 'banana', 'kiwi', 'dragonfruit']
>>> years = [2012, 2013, 2014, 2015]
>>> students_in_class = [30, 22, 28, 33]
>>>
>>> print(fruit[0])
apple
>>>
>>>
>>> print(fruit[3])
dragonfruit
>>>
>>>
```

For extra practice, work with the other lists that we made earlier, and try printing different items from these lists using this code sample:

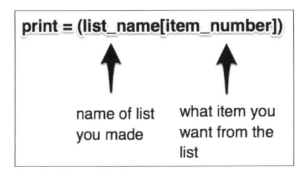

Where the code says `list_name`, write the name of the list you want to use. Where the code says `item_number`, write the number of the item you want to print. Remember that lists begin counting at 0.

Changing the list – adding and removing information

Even though lists keep their order, they can be changed. Items can be added to a list, removed from them, or changed in them. Again, there are many ways to interact with lists. We will only discuss a few here, but you can always read the Python documentation for more information.

Adding items to the list

To add an item to our `fruit` list, for example, we can use a method called `list.append()`. To use this method, type the name of the list, a dot, the method name `append`, and then parentheses with the item you would like to add inside. If the item is a string, remember to use single quotes. Type the following code to add `orange` to the list of fruits we have made:

```
fruit.append('orange')
```

Then, print the list of fruit to check whether `orange` has been added to the list:

```
print(fruit)
```

```
Type "help", "copyright", "credits" or "license" for more information.
>>>
>>>
>>> fruit = ['apple', 'banana', 'kiwi', 'dragonfruit']
>>> years = [2012, 2013, 2014, 2015]
>>> students_in_class = [30, 22, 28, 33]
>>>
>>> print(fruit[0])
apple
>>>
>>>
>>> print(fruit[3])
dragonfruit
>>>
>>>
>>> fruit.append('orange')
>>> print(fruit)
['apple', 'banana', 'kiwi', 'dragonfruit', 'orange']
>>>
>>>
```

Removing items from the list

Now, let's say that we no longer want dragonfruit to appear on our list. We will use a method called list.remove(). To do this, we will type the name of our list, a dot, the remove method name , and the name of the item that we wish to remove:

```
fruit.remove('dragonfruit')
```

Then, print the list, confirm that dragonfruit has been removed:

```
print(fruit)
```

```
Type "help", "copyright", "credits" or "license" for more information.
>>>
>>>
>>> fruit = ['apple', 'banana', 'kiwi', 'dragonfruit']
>>> years = [2012, 2013, 2014, 2015]
>>> students_in_class = [30, 22, 28, 33]
>>>
>>> print(fruit[0])
apple
>>>
>>>
>>> print(fruit[3])
dragonfruit
>>>
>>>
>>> fruit.append('orange')
>>> print(fruit)
['apple', 'banana', 'kiwi', 'dragonfruit', 'orange']
>>>
>>> fruit.remove('dragonfruit')
>>> print(fruit)
['apple', 'banana', 'kiwi', 'orange']
>>>
>>>
```

If you have more than one of the same item in the list, list.remove() will only remove the first instance of that item. The other items with the same name need to be removed separately.

Lists and loops

Lists and for loops work very well together. With lists, we can do something called an **iteration**. By itself, the word *iteration* means repeating a process. We know that for loops repeat things for a limited and specific number of times. So, we can use for loops to iterate over lists of items.

In this sample, we have three colors in our list. Make this list in your Python shell:

```
colors = ['green', 'yellow', 'red']
```

Using our list, we may decide that for each color in the list, we want to print the statement I see and add each color in our list. By using the for loop with the colors list, we can type the print statement once and three sentences will be returned. Type the following for loop in your Python shell:

```
for color in colors:
    print('I see  ' + color  +  '.')
```

You will notice that, in the second line of code, we add the strings together using the plus sign operator (+). The first string, I see, starts each sentence. The second string, color, comes from the variable that we made when we wrote the for loop. The third string is a period (.) to end the sentence. Once you are done typing the print line and you press *Enter* twice, your for loop will start running, and you should see the following statements printed in your Python shell:

```
I see green.
I see yellow.
I see red.
```

Notice that the sentences print the colors in the order that they appear in the list. Order is preserved in lists:

```
Last login: Sun Dec 13 22:01:11 on ttys001
Jessicas-MacBook-Air-2:~ jessicanickel$ python3.5
Python 3.5.0 (v3.5.0:374f501f4567, Sep 12 2015, 11:00:19)
[GCC 4.2.1 (Apple Inc. build 5666) (dot 3)] on darwin
Type "help", "copyright", "credits" or "license" for more information.
>>>
>>>
>>>
>>> colors = ['green', 'yellow', 'red']
>>>
>>> for color in colors:
...     print('I see ' + str(color) + '.')
...
I see green.
I see yellow.
I see red.
>>>
>>>
```

As you can imagine, lists and `for` loops are very powerful when used together. Instead of having to type the line three times with three different pieces of code, we only had to type two lines of code.

Our `for` loop, with only those two lines of code, would work if there were twenty colors or even two hundred colors in the list. We will explore the power of using lists more in the next chapter and mini-game.

Dictionaries

Dictionaries are a different way to organize data. At first glance, a dictionary may look just like a list. However, dictionaries have different jobs, rules, and different syntax than lists.

Parts of a dictionary like lists, dictionaries have different parts that need to be used to make them work—names, use curly braces to store information. For example, if we wanted to make a dictionary called `numbers`, we would put the dictionary entries inside curly braces. Here is a simple example to type into your Python shell:

```
numbers = {'one': 1, 'two': 2, 'three': 3}
```

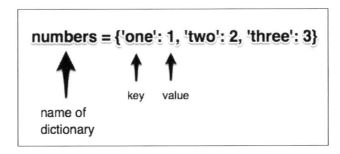

Key/value pairs in dictionaries

As you can see in the previous screenshot, the dictionary stores information with things called **keys** and **values**. In a dictionary of items, for example, we might have keys that tell us the names of each item and values that tell us how many of each item we have in our inventory. Once we store these items in our dictionary, we can add or remove new items (keys), add new amounts (values), or change the amounts of existing items. If you have ever used a contact list in your e-mail or a smartphone, you might recognize that it matches a key (the person's name) with a value (their e-mail ID or phone number). Keys and values do not always have to be in the form of strings and integers, but for our next example, we will use a dictionary to store all the items that a video game hero might have on a quest.

The following is an example of a dictionary that can hold some information for a game. Let's suppose that the hero in our game has some items that are needed to survive. Here is a dictionary of our hero's items; type this dictionary of items into your Python shell:

```
items = {'arrows' : 200, 'rocks' : 25, 'food' : 15, 'lives' : 2}
```

Now we have a dictionary that gives us information about the items that our hero has. Unlike a list, a dictionary does not keep items in the order that they were entered. You can see this by printing out a small dictionary a few times and noticing the results. To print a dictionary, we type `print`, and then we place the name of the dictionary in the print statement:

```
print(items)
```

You will notice that the output of the code results in the dictionary being printed in a different order from how you entered it. There is a possibility that it might print the same order, but it is more likely to print differently than how you entered it. Take a look at this screenshot for an example:

```
>>> items = {'arrows':200, 'rocks':25, 'food':15, 'lives':2}
>>> print(items)
{'food': 15, 'lives': 2, 'arrows': 200, 'rocks': 25}
```

So, our dictionary has keys such as `arrows`, `rocks`, `food`, and `lives`. Each of the numbers that is stored as a value tells us the number of items that our hero has. To find out the value of a key, we use a `print` statement that contains the `items` dictionary name with the `arrows` key . Notice that the `arrows` key is placed in square brackets. The syntax is important. Type the following code in your Python shell to return the value of `arrows`:

```
print(items['arrows'])
```

The result of this `print` statement should output `200` as this is the number of arrows our hero has in their inventory:

```
Last login: Mon Dec  7 16:39:41 on ttys000
Jessicas-MacBook-Air-2:~ jessicanickel$ python3.5
Python 3.5.0 (v3.5.0:374f501f4567, Sep 12 2015, 11:00:19)
[GCC 4.2.1 (Apple Inc. build 5666) (dot 3)] on darwin
Type "help", "copyright", "credits" or "license" for more information.
>>>
>>>
>>>
>>> items = {'arrows': 200, 'rocks': 25, 'food': 15, 'lives':2}
>>>
>>> print(items['arrows'])
200
>>>
>>>
```

Changing the dictionary – adding and removing information

Python has several ways of interacting with dictionary data. There are many functions that we can use. For now, we will focus on those functions that allow us to add and remove things from our dictionaries.

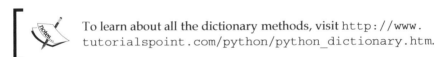 To learn about all the dictionary methods, visit `http://www.tutorialspoint.com/python/python_dictionary.htm`.

Adding items to the dictionary

Consider a situation where, in our game, we allow the player to discover and collect fireballs later in the game. To add an item to the dictionary, we will use what is called the **subscript** method to add a new key and new value to our dictionary.

To create a subscript, we will use the name of the dictionary. Then, in square brackets, we write the name of the item (key) that we wish to add. The item is a string type, so it needs to be in single quotes. Finally, we will set the value to how many of the item (key) that we want to put into our dictionary. To add fireballs to your dictionary, copy the following code in your Python shell:

```
items['fireball'] = 10
```

If we print the entire dictionary of items, you will see that the `fireball` has been added. Type this code in your Python shell:

```
print(items)
```

Your outcome should include the `fireball` as one of the items. Remember, however, that your code may not be in the same order as the code in this book because dictionaries do not remember orders:

```
Last login: Mon Dec  7 16:39:41 on ttys000
Jessicas-MacBook-Air-2:~ jessicanickel$ python3.5
Python 3.5.0 (v3.5.0:374f501f4567, Sep 12 2015, 11:00:19)
[GCC 4.2.1 (Apple Inc. build 5666) (dot 3)] on darwin
Type "help", "copyright", "credits" or "license" for more information.
>>>
>>>
>>>
>>> items = {'arrows': 200, 'rocks': 25, 'food': 15, 'lives':2}
>>>
>>> print(items['arrows'])
200
>>>
>>> items['fireball'] = 10
>>>
>>> print(items)
{'rocks': 25, 'lives': 2, 'fireball': 10, 'arrows': 200, 'food': 15}
>>>
```

Changing the value of an existing item

We can also change the value of the keys in our dictionary. Suppose, for example, that our hero is collecting rocks in the game and then loses the rocks because they use them to build a rock wall. How would our game keep track of each rock added to or removed from the game inventory?

The `dict.update()` method allows us to alter the values of keys in the dictionary. For our dictionary, we will be changing the value of rocks as our hero collects or uses the rocks. To use `dict.update()`, we replace `dict` with the name of our dictionary, which is `items`. Then, in `()`, we use `{}` to type the name of the item whose value we wish to update.

We use a colon (:) and then write the new number of items that we want to see in the dictionary. Try this in your Python shell:

```
items.update({'rocks':10})

print(items)
```

```
Last login: Sun Dec 13 22:06:25 on ttys001
Jessicas-MacBook-Air-2:~ jessicanickel$ python3.5
Python 3.5.0 (v3.5.0:374f501f4567, Sep 12 2015, 11:00:19)
[GCC 4.2.1 (Apple Inc. build 5666) (dot 3)] on darwin
Type "help", "copyright", "credits" or "license" for more information.
>>>
>>> items = {'arrows': 200, 'rocks': 25, 'food': 15, 'lives':2}
>>>
>>> items.update({'rocks':10})
>>>
>>> print(items)
{'food': 15, 'lives': 2, 'arrows': 200, 'rocks': 10}
>>>
>>>
```

You will notice that if you have performed the print(items) function, you will now have 10 rocks instead of 25. We have now successfully updated our number of items.

Removing items from the dictionary

To remove something from a dictionary, you must reference the key or the name of the item, and then delete the item. By doing so, the value that goes with the item will also be removed since the key and value are paired.

In Python, the del statement can be used to remove a key/value pair from the dictionary. This means using del along with the name of the dictionary and the name of the item (key) that you wish to remove.

Let's use the items dictionary as our example. We will use the del statement, the name of the items dictionary, and the name of the lives key that's placed inside of the square brackets. Hence, we can use a print statement to test and check whether the lives key was removed along with the value of lives, which is 2:

```
del items['lives']

print(items)
```

If your `del` statement worked, the `lives` key is no longer in the dictionary and neither is the number of `lives`, which was 2. This is similar to taking a word out of a printed dictionary. If you removed the word, you would need to remove the definition as well. The items list will now look like this:

```
>>>
>>> del items['lives']
>>>
>>> print(items)
{'food': 15, 'arrows': 200, 'rocks': 10}
>>>
>>>
```

With dictionaries, information is stored and retrieved differently than in lists, but we can still perform the same operations of adding and removing information as well as making changes to the information.

List or dictionary

You have learned about two great Python data structures, lists and dictionaries. Now, we need to know when to use these tools. While both tools store information, they do so in very different ways. Let's compare these two structures so that we can better understand how each structure can be used.

Lists are good to use when we want to keep track of items and need to remember the order of those items. We use a lot of lists in everyday life that meet these criteria.

Some examples of lists are as follows:

- A grocery list with different food items
- A list of song titles in an MP3 player
- A list of fiction book titles that are available in a library
- A list of items that are available for purchase on a website

Each of these things has an order as a desirable characteristic, and items can be added or removed from the lists. If we wanted to write a short program in Python to keep track of our fiction book titles or find songs in an MP3 playlist, a list might be a good place to start.

Lists can be used with loops to do a lot of powerful things. Some of these include making lists that create themselves using loops (yes, really) or making lists from lots of user input. Lists are slower to search because they're automatically searched from the beginning.

A dictionary is more useful when data does not need order but needs to be paired with something else. For example, perhaps you own fiction and nonfiction books, and you want to write a program that stores the title, author, and the genre. Using a dictionary would be better for this task so that you can quickly figure out the author of a book based on its title or for all the fiction books that you own. You can also interact with your dictionary to make changes. Also, dictionaries can be searched very quickly because they do not need to be searched from the beginning.

An example of a dictionary that is used in programming is a *Thesaurus*. This is a dictionary of lists.

A quick task for you

Now that you are familiar with lists and dictionaries, here is a quick task for you to review your knowledge.

Q1. What is the proper syntax to use when creating a dictionary?

1. ( )
2. { }
3. " "
4. [ ]

Q2. What kinds of data can be included in one list?

1. Strings only
2. Floats only
3. Integers and floats
4. All datatypes can be included a list

Q3. What is the proper syntax to use when creating a list?

1. ( )
2. { }
3. " "
4. [ ]

Summary

In this chapter, you learned how to create your own lists and dictionaries. You also tried to perform some basic operations with lists and dictionaries, including how to add and remove data. Finally, you learned the syntax differences between lists and dictionaries as well as the optimal uses of lists and dictionaries.

In the next chapter, we are going to move forward and make a game called *What's in my backpack?* This game will be a simple, two-player game that will ask both users to put some objects into a backpack and then allow each user to guess what is in the other user's backpack.

We will write code to add items to a list, keep track of usernames, items, and scores in a list and dictionary, and then use a `for` loop to keep track of the game. There are a lot of moving parts in our next game, and it will be a lot of fun to make something that has two players! Are you ready? Let's go!

What's in Your Backpack?

In *Chapter 6*, *Working with Data – Lists and Dictionaries*, we explored how to store, retrieve, and change data using lists and dictionaries in Python. In this chapter, we will build a two player game called **What's in Your Backpack?** This game will require us to review all of the skills we have learned since the beginning of this book. We use our skills to make loops, ask for information from the user with the `raw_input()` function, and then store this information in lists or dictionaries.

Be prepared to also learn some new skills that might seem complicated. We will try something called **nesting** or putting one thing inside another. With nesting lists and dictionaries, we have more flexible data storage. Using this new nesting skill with the other skills we have learned, we will create a game that can be played by two users or adjusted to be played by many users.

Setting up our coding environment

This chapter will have the largest amount of code that we have written. Since we are going to do a lot of coding, it is important to have our tools ready so that we can test run our code frequently and save often.

> Testing and saving the code as you go along allows you to try new things and correct any mistakes!

To work on this game, it is recommended that you have your Python shell open so that you can test out small lines of code before putting them into your text editor.

Also, you will need to open your text editor (JEdit in Mac/Linux or Notepad++ in Windows), and make a new file called `backpack.py`. Finally, you will need to open your command prompt so that you can run the `backpack.py` program to test it out while you are writing the game. Hopefully, you are feeling more at ease with the different tools that are used to create a computer program. If you do not recall how to open the Python shell or command prompt, refer to *Chapter 1, Welcome! Let's Get Started.*

If you have questions or want to know more about the Python shell, command prompt, or text editor that you are using on your computer, perform an Internet search and learn more about the tools.

To learn about the tools, documentation, and the advanced techniques used in this book, you can refer to the following links:

`http://www.jedit.org/`

`https://notepad-plus-plus.org/`

`https://docs.python.org/3.5/library/idle.html`

`http://www.macworld.co.uk/feature/mac-software/get-more-out-of-os-x-terminal-3608274/`

`http://windows.microsoft.com/en-US/windows-vista/Open-a-Command-Prompt-window`

Planning to program your game

Before we dive right into programming, we need to think critically about what we are building and plan a bit ahead of time; this helps us figure out what programming skills we need to use in order to make our program work.

So, let's imagine this game with each player having their own virtual backpack:

- Each player enters their name, and then places four items in their backpack.
- Then, each player gets a chance to guess what is in the other player's backpack.
- If the player guesses correctly, a message is printed, and one point is added to the score.
- If the player guesses incorrectly, a different message is printed, and no points are added to the score.

- Finally, a message asks the players whether they would like to play the game again.
- If they type yes, the whole process takes place again. If they type no, then the scores of each player are printed and the entire game stops.

Already, we have many things to do. Each of the points mentioned is a task that needs to be solved using our coding skills. Before reading the code sample ahead, ask yourself how you would try to solve each problem. Maybe make some drawings, or type an outline of each thing that the program needs to do to succeed. Then, save those ideas as you go through this chapter and write your backpack game. You might try some of your ideas, and check whether your ideas work! If so, that is great. You will discover that there is not one *proper* way to program. Some ways are better than others, but it is never wrong to try something out.

Skills needed to make a program

Now, we will review our list of elements needed to make a successful game, and we will brainstorm the solutions to program each element. Taking time now to figure out how we want to solve the problem helps us create a program that works well once the pieces are put together.

Each player enters their name, and then places four items in their backpack. In order to get the player names into the computer, we will need to make a variable to hold the name of each player. We will use raw_input() to get the items and store the items in the computer:

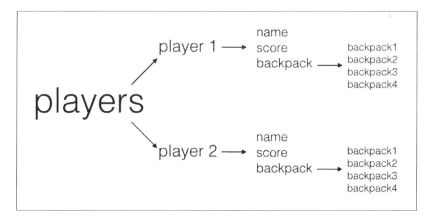

Each player gets a chance to guess what is in the other player's backpack.

Remember our game Higher or Lower? This function will be like higher and lower. We will compare the first player's guesses to the items in the second player's backpack. We will need to use `raw_input` to do prompt the guesses. Then, we will need some `if/elif/else` logic to compare the guesses and give the user output. The output will be printed to the screen using `print`.

If the player guesses correctly, a message is printed, and one point is added to the score.

If the player guesses incorrectly, a different message is printed, and no points are added to the score.

Score, play again, or quit?

When a player wins or uses up all of their guesses, we will use the `if/elif/else` logic to output a message that asks the players whether they would like to play the game again.

If player types `yes`, the game runs again.

If a player types `no`, then the scores of each player are printed and the game stops running.

Getting and storing player information

Our first task is to figure out how we are going to get and store information from those who play our game. There are a few steps we need to take, including asking the player for their name, and then storing the player's name. We will also perform some code in the background to store information about the player that we have not yet asked for. This is a sneaky bit of coding that is quite fun and will let you expand your game if you want to. Let's walk through each step.

Making a players list

The first thing that we will do is make an empty list to store information about each player. We are going to name the list `players`, but we are not going to put anything in our list yet. Why not? Well, our players might be different in each game, and they will have different information too, so we need to allow our game to store this information as our players enter it into the computer. Here is what the `players` list looks like:

```
players = []
```

Now that we have made this list, we can add players to this list. Recall that we will also make a profile to store information about the players. In fact, the profile will be stored in some tiny dictionaries that we make inside the lists!

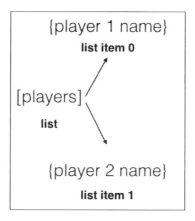

New skill! Putting one item inside another item. This is called **nesting**. Next, we will learn how to nest a dictionary inside of a list.

Player profiles

In this next step, we are going to make a dictionary for each player. The dictionary that we make will have placeholders for the player name, the player's backpack items, and the player's score:

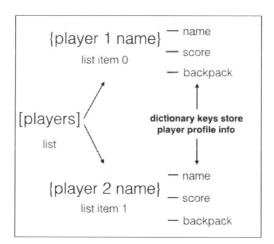

Imagine that all of the information in the dictionary is a `player` profile. The `player` profile will be filled in by information that we get from the player's interactions with our game. The code in the following screenshot is what the completed code for our players will look like:

```
1  # getting information about the players
2  # storing the information about the players
3
4
5  players = []
6
7  for i in range(2):
8      players.append({
9          "name": "",
10         "score": 0,
11         "backpack": []
12     })
13
```

Before you write any code, let's read and break down the code. The first two lines are comments to remind us of what we are doing, and line 5 is where we make an empty list. The code in line 7, which is the first line of code that the computer cares about, allows us to do the following:

- Set the number of players with the `range()` function: Since counting in Python starts at zero, and the `range()` function does not include the last number, we are creating profiles for `player 0` and `player 1` (refer to *Chapter 6, Working with Data – Lists and Dictionaries*, where we spent time printing and counting lists, to refresh your memory about how lists items are counted).

- The `for` loop to make profile for each player: For `player 0` and `player 1`, we will make a player profile with information.

- The `player.append()` function: This adds an information type to each player profile. In this case, name is `string`, score is `int`, and backpack is an `empty` list.

The `backpack` dictionary key is special because it is a list that will store all of the backpack items inside of the profile. It allows the user to have many items stored in the same place:

```
1  # getting information about the players
2  # storing the information about the players
3
4
5  players = []
6
7  for profile in range(2):      # <--- run loop to create each player.
8      players.append({          # <-- adds dictionary of placeholders to 'players' list
9          "name": "",           # <-- placeholder string stores name of each player
10         "score": 0,           # <-- starts at 0
11         "backpack": []        # <-- empty list stores items in each player's backpack
12     })
```

Player profiles – how do they work?

Now, let's think about all the information in a player profile. We have a list called
players. Inside the players list, we have a dictionary for each player. The dictionary
is where the player profile information is stored. Inside the dictionary for each player,
we have made room for an item list. The item list is called backpack, and its job is to
remember all the list items in the player profile. Try to imagine the profile like a tree
that has more leaves as it breaks away from the trunk and branch:

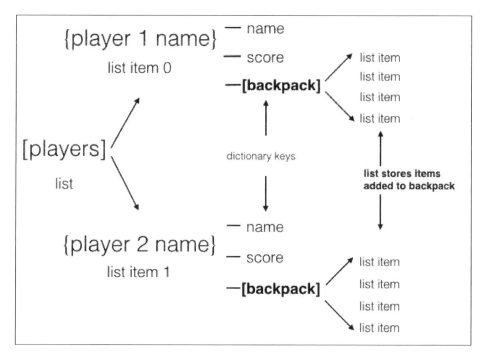

The name for what we have done is called **nesting**. Nesting is when we put one thing inside something else. Here, we have nested one datatype (a dictionary) inside another datatype (players list).

 Save your code if you have not done so already!

Add players to profile

So, we have set up a data structure, called the **player** profile, as a way to store the information about each player. Now, we need to write the code that will prompt the players to enter their information into our program. We will use the raw_input() function to get information from the players and store this information in the user profile. Our request for user information will continue inside the for loop.

First, read through the code from lines 15-20 in this screenshot:

```
1  # getting information about the players
2  # storing the information about the players
3
4
5  players = []
6
7  for i in range(2):        # <-- run loop for the correct number of players.
8      players.append({      # <-- add dictionary of name, score, backpack to 'players'
9          "name": "",       # <-- is empty to accept name of each player
10         "score": 0,       # <-- starts at 0
11         "backpack": []    # <-- lists the items in each player's backpack
12     })
13
14
15     players[i]["name"] = input("Enter name for player " + str(i + 1) + ": ")
16     print("Enter four (4) items to put into your backpack.")
17     for j in range(4):
18         backpack_item = input("Item name: ")
19         players[i]["backpack"].append(backpack_item)
20     # print(players[i]["backpack"])
21
```

In line 15 of this code, you will notice our raw_input() command, which asks the player to enter their name. Did you notice that the name dictionary key is used? Did you notice that before the name key, players[i] is used? This means that the answer to the Enter your name prompt will be stored in the dictionary under the name key. A player profile will be created, and it will be waiting for information about the backpack items and the game score.

The player number is being set by `i`. The lowercase `i` represents one player. So, line 15 asks us for the name of player `i`. How does it know what number to choose? Where is `i` getting that information? If you go back up to the `for` loop, you will notice `for i in range(2)`. This means *for the first player of two players*, do all the things in the loop. When line 15 runs the `for` loop the first time, it asks for input from `player 1`; when the `for` loop runs the second time, it asks for input from `player 2`. A `for` loop with a `range(2)` only runs twice, so after getting and storing input from `player 2`, the `for` loop stops looping.

Adding items to the virtual backpack

Now that we have added the player's name, we want to add four items to the player's virtual backpack. The virtual backpack is really a list inside the dictionary. We will store the list of each player's items in their virtual backpack, which is inside each player's profile. Asking a player to answer the same question multiple times presents a new programming challenge. How will we limit our program to ask for only four items? How will we add each item to the backpack of the correct player?

Limiting items in a virtual backpack

To make sure that we only add four items to each virtual backpack, we are using another `for` loop (inside our first `for` loop). The inside loop says `for item in range(4)`. This means *for each item out of four items*, do all the things in the loop. In our backpack loop, this means that we will enter items 0, 1, 2, and 3 into the backpack using the `raw_input()` function.

In the `players[i]backpack` dictionary, we append (add) items to the list inside of the backpack by using `append(backpack_item)`. Because we want four items, our `for` loop runs four times after asking for the name and items of the player. When this `backpack_item` code finishes running, the entire player loop will begin again, asking for the name and items for the second player. In this process, we get the information we need to fill out the player profiles that are stored in the dictionaries of `player 1` and `player 2`:

```
11        "backpack": []   # <-- empty list stores items in each player's backpack
12    })
13
14
15    players[profile]["name"] = raw_input("Enter name for player " + str(profile + 1) + ": ")
16    print("Enter four (4) items to put into your backpack.")
17    for item in range(4):
18        backpack_item = raw_input("Item name: ")
19        players[profile]["backpack"].append(backpack_item)
20    # print(players[profile]["backpack"])
```

To review, when you run your code, you should expect to see the following:

1. Create a name and profile of `player 1`—`Enter name for player 1`.

2. Ask `player 1` to put items in their backpack—`Enter 4 items to put into your backpack`.

3. Player enters four items.

4. Create a name and profile `of player 2`—`Enter name for player 2`.

5. Ask `player 2` to put items in their backpack—`Enter 4 items to put into your backpack`.

Testing your code so far

You have now written all of the data storage elements of the game. Save your code again if you have not done so already, and test what you have written.

First, do a visual test of your `backpack.py` code file. Make sure that your code is indented properly. Look for syntax errors such as misplaced quotes, periods, square brackets, curly braces, and parentheses. Make sure that everything is spelled correctly. Save after each mistake that you fix.

Next, use your command prompt (Windows) or terminal (Mac/Linux) to test your code by running your program. When you run your program, you should expect to be asked to enter the name of player 1, enter four items, enter the name of player 2, and enter four more items:

```
Enter name for player 1: Jessica
Enter four (4) items to put into your backpack.
Item name: apple
Item name: pear
Item name: banana
Item name: grape
Enter name for player 2: Jose
Enter four (4) items to put into your backpack.
Item name: cup
Item name: plate
Item name: fork
Item name: knife
Jessicas-MacBook-Air-2:Desktop jessicanickel$
```

If you want to make sure that the backpack items you enter are being properly stored, you can use the test code from line 20 in the screenshot. Just uncomment (erase the hashtag in front of) the code in line 20, and then run the code again. Use the print statement from line 20 to check what the computer is storing. Sometimes, the computer reads things differently than we think it will, so it is good to have a print statement to double-check your work:

```
Jessicas-MacBook-Air:Desktop jessicanickel$ python backpack.py
Enter name for player 1: Jess
Enter four (4) items to put into your backpack.
Item name: bread
Item name: pan
Item name: roti
Item name: pane
['bread', 'pan', 'roti', 'pane']
Enter name for player 2: David
Enter four (4) items to put into your backpack.
Item name: chicken
Item name: goat
Item name: pig
Item name: lamb
['chicken', 'goat', 'pig', 'lamb']
```

If you have a mistake, you will get an error message. Usually, the error message will have a message that tells you where the problem is in the code. Look at your error messages if you do something incorrectly, and use these messages to figure out what is going wrong. When you correct an error, you can make a note or even make a comment in your code so that you recall how you fixed the problem.

A game loop

We have planned and coded how to get information from players. Now, we need to code a **game loop**. What is a game loop? The game loop keeps the game running by starting the game using user actions to update the state of the game, if necessary, and continuing to operate until the game is ended, stopping the loop.

Our game loop lets us start the game, use stored information from the players to make changes to the game state, and print outputs so that we know whether the guess was correct or incorrect or what the score is at the end of the game. Our game loop also shuts off if conditions change to stop the game. We have already used a game loop in our Higher or Lower game, and this game loop will be similar. Using the game loop, we can write the code to complete our game.

Bringing back the while loop

So, you may remember using the `while` loop back in *Chapters 4, Making Decisions: Python Control Flows*, and *Chapter 5, Loops and Logic*. We will be using the `while` loop again to set up the game loop. There is quite a lot happening in the game loop (the `while` loop), so let's take a look at it step by step. First, look at this screenshot of all of the code inside the game loop:

```
22
23 game_on = True
24 while game_on:
25     for i in range(2):
26         player_choice = raw_input(players[i]["name"] + ", guess an item from the other backpack: ")
27         other_player = players[(i+1) % 2]
28         if player_choice in other_player["backpack"]:
29             print("You guessed an item from the backpack!")
30             players[i]["score"] += 1
31         else:
32             print("You did not guess an item from the backpack.")
33
34         play_again = raw_input("Do you want to play again? Type YES or NO: ")
35         if (play_again == "NO"):
36             game_on = False
37
```

The first thing that you see is the comment telling anybody who reads the code what the code is doing. Comments are not required, but sometimes they can be helpful when you are writing a program. This comment simply tells us that the next section is the game loop.

The game loop starts with the `game_on` variable. The `game_loop` variable is set to equal `True` (remember, `True` is a Boolean). The next line says `while game_on:`; this means that *since the* `while` *loop is* `True`, *keep running the* `while` *loop until something happens to make it* `False` *(untrue)*. Since `while game_on:` is `True`, the game will keep running using the information that we gathered when the game started. The game will end only when `game_on = False`.

Inside our game loop is another `for` loop. When one loop is inside another loop, they are nested. You might notice that this `for` loop is almost the same as the `for` loop in line 7. This code runs `for i in range(2)`, which means that *for each player in the two players*, do all the things in the loop.

In this `for` loop, from line 26 to line 36, the main part of the game takes place. The things in this `for` loop include the following:

- Ask the first player to guess an item from the second player's backpack
- Print if the first player is correct or incorrect
- Add points to the first player's score if correct

- Switch to the second player
- Ask the second player to guess an item from first player's backpack
- Print if the second player is correct or incorrect
- Add points to the second player's score if correct
- Ask the players if they want to play again
- If *YES* to play again, restart the loop and redo all actions

The preceding list has all of the events that take place inside of the `for` loop, which starts in line 25 of the code. We will break down the code that makes this happen in the next section of the chapter.

Comparing guesses with backpack items

In the math chapter, we learned about something called **modulo**. Now, it is coming back. In the backpack game, we compare the items in one player's backpack to the guess of another player. Then, the players switch places! How will the computer keep track of which backpack to look at and what player should be chosen? We can use modulo to help us always choose the correct player in the two-player version of this game.

Here is the line of code that uses modulo (line 27):

```
other_player = players[(i+1) % 2]
```

This line of code uses modulo to identify the opposite player by looking for the player in the `players` list we made in line 5. Here is the basic idea:

- Erin (player 1) = 0 and Tanvir (player 2) = 1.
- Whoever is playing needs to compare their answer to the backpack of the other player.
- To get the backpack of the other player, we tell the computer *Hey, we need the backpack of the player who is NOT guessing right now.* We do this with math.
- Erin needs to use Tanvir's backpack to make guesses. Remember that Tanvir = 1.
    - $(0 + 1) \% 2 = 1$.
    - This formula says (Erin + 1) modulo 2 = Tanvir's backpack.
    - As you can see, this math formula is equal to 1, so it is asking for Tanvir's backpack.
    - Erin *WANTS* to guess what is in Tanvir's backpack, so this is correct.

- Tanvir needs to guess what is in Erin's backpack. Remember, Erin = 0.
  - (1 + 1) % 2 = 0.
  - This formula says (Tanvir + 1) modulo 2 = Erin's backpack.
  - As you can see, this formula is equal to 0, so it is asking for Erin's backpack.
  - Tanvir *WANTS* to guess what is in Erin's backpack, so this is correct.

Using the formula, we choose the player profile from the `players` list. You know we are using a list because we use the name `players`, which we defined in line 5 of the program, and we use square brackets, `[ ]`, to say which list item we want to use. Inside the square brackets, we put a math formula that is equal to one of the items in our list.

Keeping score

To keep score in the game, the following line of code is used:

```
players[i]["score"] += 1
```

You will notice a new symbol, `+=`. The `+=` symbol is a shortcut that lets us take a value (`score`), add an amount to this value (we are adding 1 point), and then make the value of `score` equal to the new value.

This line of code says that if the first player makes a match to an item in the second player backpack, then the new score for the first player is `score += 1`. You will remember that in the beginning of the game, we set each player to have a score of zero in the dictionary. Now, we are updating that score to be `score += 1`. Each time the first player scores, `score` will be updated by 1, and the computer will remember the new score.

Ending the game

Once we are tired of playing the game, we can answer the question *Do you want to play again? Type YES or NO:* with NO. Once we do this, you will notice that `game_on = False` appears in the code to stop the `while` loop. As soon as the loop stops, the last line of code is executed:

```
37
38  for player in players:
39      print(player["name"] + " score: " + str(player["score"]))
40
```

This line of code prints out the scores of each player only *AFTER* the game loop is completed. This line of code is outside of the `for` loop and the game loop. If you only ran the game once, the highest score could only be one. However, if you ran the game five or ten times, then your high scores could be as high as five or ten, depending on how many items each player guessed correctly.

Testing your game

Now, the moment of truth! First, look at each line of code. Check for indentation errors and syntax errors. Once you have proofread your code, save your work. When you are ready, run your code and play the game against yourself to see whether your code works. Run your code using your command prompt (Windows) or your terminal (Mac/Linux).

The expected behavior is that each player will get one chance to guess the contents of the other player's backpack. Then, you will be asked whether you would like to continue. If you press yes, the guessing will start again. If you press no, then the scores will print and the game will stop:

- If your game is working the way you expect it to, you can show it to someone else and see how it works for them
- Print out different messages for correct or incorrect guesses
- Make an ending message, such as *Thanks for playing*

These are just a few of many ways that you can change the game. By playing with the code, you can learn more about how it behaves, and gain a greater understanding of why and how things work. You are encouraged to play the game many times, by yourself and with others, to get ideas about how you might change your code to alter the game as well as understand each line of code thoroughly.

A quick task for you

Q1. What is nesting?

1. When birds build a home
2. When one item is inside another item
3. When a game loop is used
4. When a dictionary is used

Q2. What does the list called `players` organize in this game?

1. It organizes a scores
2. It organizes player names
3. It organizes all the items belonging to each player
4. It organizes a backpack

Q3. What kind of item is inside the `players` list?

1. Any item that the player wants
2. A string
3. An integer
4. A dictionary

Q4. What is a game loop?

1. A loop that keeps going forever
2. A loop that holds the logic of the game
3. A loop that keeps the game running
4. 2 and 3

Summary

This chapter has been a lot of work. We reviewed almost every skill that we learned so far! We used logic in our `if`/`else` statements. We used Booleans, such as `True` and `False`, to change our game state. We ran `for` loops to control how many times certain events too place, and we ran a `while` loop as our game loop. Finally, we used *lists* and *dictionaries* to store customized information and to allow for information, such as the player score, to be changed during the game. We learned a new skill in this chapter: *nesting*. Our backpack game used nested lists and dictionaries. We also used nested loops, such as our `while` loop, with the `for` loop inside.

This chapter used one of many ways to make this game. Our purpose was to use all of the tools we have in our Python toolbox. There are many different ways to make a **backpack** game. Some might be simpler, others might be more complicated. Something to explore before you go on is to try and make a variation of this game before you go on. You can use this code as a starting point, and use Internet searches and other books by Packt Publishing to help sharpen your Python skills.

In the next chapter, we are going to learn about making graphics using Python. We will learn some features of the graphics library that we can apply to develop our final game. Some of the features that we will learn include how to make a game screen, draw shapes, and move things around. We will even learn how to make one object bounce off another (hint: it's an illusion!). The next chapter will also require some software installation, which may require you to have password access to your computer.

8
pygame

In the previous chapter, we got to use every skill we learned in the book to create a simple, two-player guessing game. In this chapter, you will learn about pygame modules and how they work to make game creation possible using Python.

What is pygame?

As stated on the most current pygame website, `http://www.pygame.org/hifi. html`, *pygame is a set of Python modules designed for writing games*. **pygame**, like Python, is free and open source, meaning that it can be used for free and shared with others. The developers of pygame have made sure that it is compatible with several different graphics display engines, so this means that the games developed using pygame could be played in a variety of environments. Installing pygame is a careful process, and you may need the help of your parents or another adult since there are a few steps. We will discuss the installation for Windows, Mac, and Linux in the next section of the chapter.

pygame is quite popular, and the website is undergoing revisions at the time of writing this. Sometimes, you will see an older part of the site, while other times, you will see a new part of the site. New parts of the pygame website look like this:

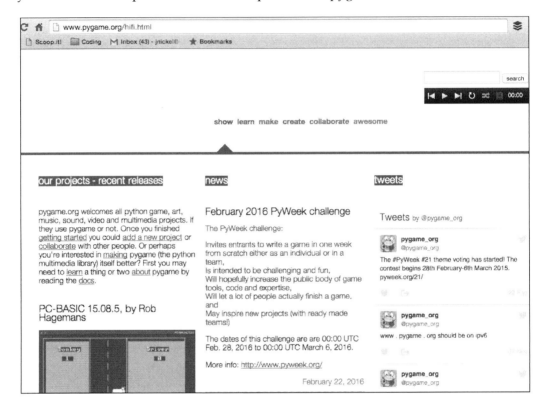

Meanwhile, older parts of the pygame website have a green background, as follows:

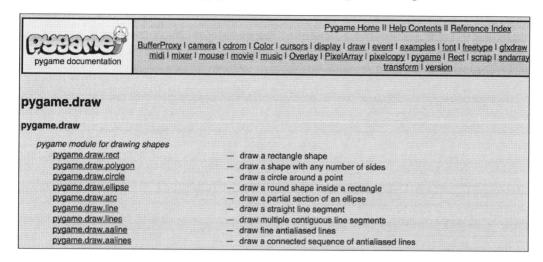

You can always use the search bar on either part of the website to locate information that you need.

Once you've installed pygame, you will learn about the features of pygame that will be the most useful for our final project, in *Chapter 9, Tiny Tennis*. Since this is our first game using visuals, we will not use all of the features offered by pygame in our first project. We will use most of the basic features that are required to make an interactive, two-player game. However, once you feel ready, you are encouraged to look at the pygame website (`http://www.pygame.org/hifi.html`), the pygame documentation (available in your installation of pygame as well as on the website), and the more advanced pygame book published by Packt Publishing, *Instant Pygame for Python Game Development How-to, Ivan Idris*, to gain a better understanding of the more complex tools that pygame offers.

Installing pygame

pygame is installed a little differently on each operating system. The next section of this chapter contains the instructions to install pygame on Windows, Mac, Linux, and Raspberry Pi systems. You can skip to the section that has instructions on how to install pygame on your operating system, and if you are not 100% sure of what you are doing, go ahead and get some help for this section. Remember that you will need an Internet connection to install pygame, and some parts of the installation may take time.

Installing pygame – Windows

To install pygame on Windows, you will need to go to http://www.pygame.org/ hifi.html. If you do not know where the Windows version of pygame is, type download in the search bar and go to the **Downloads** page. You should see a screen with this information:

Windows

Get the version of pygame for your version of python. You may need to uninstall old versions of pygame first.
NOTE: if you had pygame 1.7.1 installed already, please uninstall it first. Either using the uninstall feature - or remove the files: c:\python25\lib\site-packages\pygame . We changed the type of installer, and there will be issues if you don't uninstall pygame 1.7.1 first (and all old versions).

- pygame-1.9.1.win32-py2.7.msi 3.1MB
- pygame-1.9.1release.win32-py2.4.exe 3MB
- pygame-1.9.1release.win32-py2.5.exe 3MB
- pygame-1.9.1.win32-py2.5.msi 3MB
- pygame-1.9.1.win32-py2.6.msi 3MB
- pygame-1.9.2a0.win32-py2.7.msi 6.4MB
- pygame-1.9.1.win32-py3.1.msi 3MB
- pygame-1.9.2a0.win32-py3.2.msi 6.4MB
- (optional) Numeric for windows python2.5 (note: Numeric is old, best to use numpy) http://rene.f0o.com/~rene/stuff/Numeric-24.2.win32-py2.5.exe
- windows 64bit users note: use the 32bit python with this 32bit pygame.

There are some pre release binaries for 64bit windows, and for python 2.7 at http://www.lfd.uci.edu/~gohlke/pythonlibs/#pygame

---

At the bottom of that screenshot, you will find the instructions for most Windows computers. Follow these instructions:

1. Visit the pygame website.

2. Download this version of pygame: pygame-1.9.2a0.win32-py2.7.msi.

3. Go to your Downloads folder.

4. Double-click on the pygame-1.9.2a0.win32-py2.7.msi file.

5. Choose **Run**:

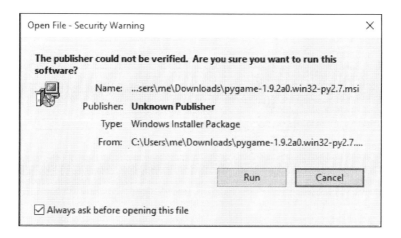

6. Choose install Python from registry option:

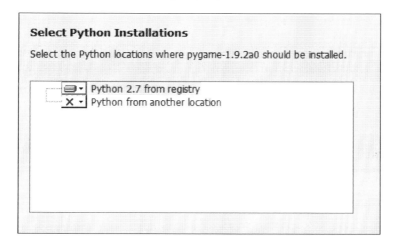

7. Allow the installation to complete.

Finally, everything should be in place. To test whether the installation worked, open your Python shell, and type this:

```
import pygame
```

If you have no error message, then your installation worked! Congratulations! If it did not work, review your steps, and don't be afraid to ask for some help.

Installing pygame – Mac

We need to do some preparatory steps to make pygame work before we actually install it on Mac. pygame requires a few dependencies or other programs to work on a Mac:

- Xcode (free, available on the App Store)
- XQuartz (free, open source)
- Homebrew (free, open source)
- An Internet connection

You may also want to get an adult to help you with the installation, especially if you are not 100% comfortable with the terminal. There are some brief instructions on the pygame Mac Wiki, located at `http://pygame.org/wiki/macintosh`.

Installing Xcode

To start, open your terminal. Go to the directory where you first installed Python (refer to *Chapter 1, Welcome! Let's Get Started*, if you have forgotten how to get to your home directory). Once you are in your Python directory, you will install Xcode. Xcode is a developer tool that has a lot of power, far beyond what we will do in this book. If you are curious about Xcode, you can find the documentation at `https://developer.apple.com/xcode/`.

For now, we will install Xcode by typing this into the terminal/command prompt:

```
xcode-select --install
```

If your computer already has Xcode installed, you will get an error message that says it is already installed. If not, then Xcode will begin installing. Once Xcode is installed, you can move on to the next step. Be patient, as Xcode takes some time to install. To test whether the install worked, try entering the install command again. You will see that it is already installed:

```
Jessicas-MacBook-Air:~ jessicanickel$ xcode-select --install
xcode-select: error: command line tools are already installed, use "Software Upd
ate" to install updates
```

Installing Homebrew

The next step is installing a package management system called Homebrew. This sounds complicated, but all it means is that you are going to be able to get cool stuff much more easily. Python has something called `pip`, and this installs Python packages. We are going to install another system called `homebrew`. Homebrew is used to manage many packages of different kinds, and it can also be used to troubleshoot.

Here is how to install homebrew using the `curl` command:

```
ruby -e "$(curl -fsSL https://raw.githubusercontent.com/Homebrew/install/
master/install
```

The preceding code should be typed in one command. The text will wrap on its own if it needs more room in your terminal. Once you type that command, the `homebrew` installation will begin. Homebrew asks you questions and gives good installation suggestions along every step, so pay attention and it should work well. For more information, you can go to the homebrew website for instructions:

```
brew.sh
```

Installing programs with homebrew

Once homebrew is installed, you can use it to install the rest of the dependencies needed to install pygame. We need to have access to Mercurial and Git. Both of these are version control systems, so every time code is changed, they keep track:

```
brew install mercurial
brew install git
brew install sdl sdl_image sdl_mixer sdl_ttf portmidi
```

These packages will take a few minutes to install, and that's okay. Once they have completed installing, then you will finally be able to install pygame. The command to install pygame uses something called `sudo` at the beginning, and you will need to know your computer's administrative password to use it.

 If you do not know the password to your computer, find a person who does.

```
sudo pip3 install hg+ http://bitbucket.org/pygame/pygame
```

Once this is installed, you should be ready to use pygame. Before we go any further, let's test it out. Open a Python shell, and in the Python shell, type the following:

```
import pygame
```

If you notice `import error: no module named pygame`, on your screen, then something has gone wrong with your installation. Check your installation, and don't be afraid to ask for some help if you need to. If nothing happens when you hit *Enter*, then the installation of pygame is correct!

Installing pygame – Ubuntu Linux

These installation instructions are for the newest version of Ubuntu Linux at the time of writing this, which is version 15.04. First, you will want to install the `pip` package manager, if it is not installed already:

```
sudo apt-get install python-pip
```

You will notice that `sudo` is used again, and this means that you will need the administrative password for your computer. Next, we will use `apt-get` to install pygame:

```
sudo apt-get install python-pygame
```

Now, to test and check whether pygame is installed correctly, you will open a Python shell and type this command:

```
import pygame
```

If there is an error message, it means that something about your installation is not correct. Reread the installation instructions and try again. Don't be afraid to ask for help if you need to. If you have an empty line following the import pygame, it means that everything is working and you are ready to move on to the next section!

Installing pygame – Raspberry Pi

If you are working with Raspberry Pi and using one of the operating systems for the Pi, you are all set! Python and pygame are preinstalled on these systems. You can learn the basic pygame functions and modules by reading the rest of this chapter.

pygame

To test the pygame functions, open your text editor, create a file called `sample.py`, and save this file in your work folder. Once you have created this file, you are ready to start learning pygame. To use pygame, we will import the pygame module in the first line of our `sample.py` file:

```
import pygame
```

Initializing pygame

Next, we need to take a look at the methods that we need in order to start our instance of pygame. To start pygame, we need to initialize an instance of all the pygame modules. We do this by calling the `init()` function:

```
pygame.init()
```

A pygame game loop is the same as the game loops that we used in previous projects. In this chapter, it will be a `while` loop that uses `while True` in order to indicate that the game loop should repeat itself over and over again until it is stopped:

```
1 import pygame
2
3 pygame.init()
4
```

Setting up the game screen – size

Once we have pygame set up and initialized, we will want to know how to make a basic background screen. First, you will learn how to set the size of our screen. Then, you will learn to set the background color. pygame has modules to do both, as well as more advanced things, with the background.

For the tasks in this section, we will use the `pygame.display` and `pygame.Surface` modules. Our first task is to set the display size. For this task, we will create a `screen_width` and `screen_height` variable, and use the `pygame.display.set_mode()` function. Write these three lines of code under `pygame.init()`:

```
screen_width = 400
screen_height = 600
pygame.display.set_mode((screen_width, screen_height))
```

This is the most basic way to set a display and pygame will be able to choose the number of colors that are best for our system if we just use this basic setup.

> Explore advanced background setting options at
> `https://www.pygame.org/docs/ref/display.html#pygame.display.set_mode`.

Compare your code with the code in the screenshot:

```
6 screen_width = 400
7 screen_height = 600
8 pygame.display.set_mode((screen_width, screen_height))
```

Setting up the game screen – color

First, we will create code so we can use colors throughout our game. In computer programming, colors are represented by numbers. Every color is made up of three numbers. Each number represents the saturation of red, green, and blue, in that order. You can use numbers between 0 and 255. When all numbers are 0, game_screen will be black. When all the choices are 255 (255, 255, 255), game_screen will be white, (255, 0, 0) for red, (0, 255, 0) for green, and (0, 0, 255) for blue.

Rather than using numbers repeatedly in our code, we will make a global variable for each color and use the name of the color instead. Let's add a list of global variables to our code, starting from line five of our sample.py file:

```
black = (0, 0, 0)
white = (255, 255, 255)
red = (255, 0, 0)
green = (0, 255, 0)
blue = (0, 0, 255)
```

For our next task, we will set our game surface color. In order to set the color, we use the fill() function. There are a few ways in which we can set the color of the background. We will make the game_screen = pygame.display.set_mode((screen_width, screen_height)) variable. Then, we will use the variable with the fill() function to set the screen color. Add the game_screen variable to the code in line 14 of the sample.py file:

```
game_screen = pygame.display.set_mode((screen_width, screen_height))
```

Then, add the code to fill the screen color in line 15:

```
game_screen.fill(black)
```

```
1  import pygame
2  import time
3
4  pygame.init()
5
6  black = (0, 0, 0)
7  white = (255, 255, 255)
8  red = (255, 0, 0)
9  green = (0, 255, 0)
10 blue = (0, 0, 255)
11
12 screen_width = 400
13 screen_height = 600
14 game_screen = pygame.display.set_mode((screen_width, screen_height))
15 game_screen.fill(black)
```

Making stationary objects

Now you will learn how to set stationary (still) items on the canvas. This is often called *drawing* the objects. To know where to put the objects, we need to know about grids and coordinates. If you have used grids such as an x axis and a y axis in math class, it will be helpful as we will use the same. We will use the x and y coordinates to set the location of each object on our grid.

In math class, the (0,0) coordinates are usually at the center of the grid. In pygame, the (0,0) coordinates are at the top-left hand corner of the screen. As you move from left to right along the x axis, the numbers become larger. So, for our screen that is (400, 600), our x axis starts at 0 on the left and goes all the way up to 400, which is our maximum screen width.

As you move from the top-left of the screen to the bottom-left of the screen along the y axis, the numbers increase. So, our y axis starts at 0 on the top, and as we go to the bottom of our screen, it goes to 600, which is our maximum screen height.

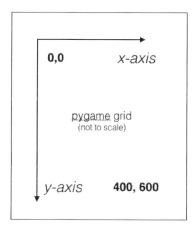

We need to know this to understand where objects will go when we draw them on the screen. In order to draw a circle in the center of the screen, for example, the center of the circle would need to fall at (200, 300). The code to draw this circle would be as follows:

```
pygame.draw.circle(Surface, color, pos, radius)
```

You can see that there are many arguments that we need to define; let's have a look at each:

- Surface would be game_screen, which identifies where to draw the circle.
- For color, we can use one of the global variables that we made for each color. In this case, we can use green.

- The `pos` argument means the position where the center of the circle will be located. Since it is (*x*, *y*), it will be two numbers in parentheses.

- The `radius` argument tells the computer the distance between the center and the edge of the circle and it is used to determine the size.

Now that you know what each argument does, let's add a circle in line 18 of the `sample.py` file:

```
pygame.draw.circle(game_screen, red, (250, 300), 20)
```

So, our preceding code will draw a red circle in the center of the main screen, which is 40 pixels wide (20 pixels from the center of the circle to the outside), with a border, which is 2 pixels wide. Then, the screen will update to show the circle.

We can draw a great number of shapes and objects using pygame, which is very suitable for making games of all kinds. We can draw rectangles, polygons, circles, and ellipses, as well as line segments of varying thicknesses and colors. The following is a screenshot of a simple circle drawn from the code we wrote. You will be able to run it as soon as we write the `while` loop:

while loop – viewing the screen

It would be great if we could see the shapes that we are drawing, so let's add some code that allows us to view our screen. We will make a `while` loop, and place all of the actions, such as drawing and making the screen, inside of the `while` loop. First, take a look at the screenshot of the `while` loop so that you can see what the finished product looks like:

```
15
16 while True:
17     pygame.draw.circle(game_screen, red, (200, 300), 20)
18     pygame.display.update()
```

You will notice that we have created a `while True` loop in line 17. This uses the `True` Boolean to keep all of the actions going while the loop is running. Add the `while` loop to line 17 of the `sample.py` file:

```
while True:
```

Beneath the `while` loop, you have already written the code to draw the circle. Indent it four spaces. On line 19, we will add the `pygame.display.update()` function:

```
pygame.display.update()
```

Now that the `while` loop is written, you should be able to run your code and see your first visual screen! To test your code, open your terminal/command prompt, and then run your code with the following command:

```
python sample.py
```

Making more shapes

Now that you know how to draw a circle, you are prepared to make other shapes. We will review the code for some basic shapes. You can add the code for different shapes to your `while loop` and make some great Python art to share with others.

Rectangle

To draw a rectangle, the basic function is `pygame.draw.rect(Surface, color (x, y, width, height))`. The `Surface` argument is `game_screen`; the color can be set to anything you like. The x and y variables will determine the placement of the top-left corner of the rectangle. The width and height determine the size of the rectangle in pixels. To add a rectangle to your code, copy this line into your `sample.py` file on line 18:

```
pygame.draw.rect(game_screen, blue, (20, 20, 50, 80))
```

Place the code *before* the `pygame.display.update()` code. The `pygame.display.update()` function should be the last line of code in your file for this exercise.

Ellipse

We can draw an ellipse by using the `pygame.draw.ellipse(Surface, color, (x, y, width, height))` function. You will notice that the `ellipse` function accepts the same arguments as the `rectangle` function, except the ellipse will draw a circle within the rectangle instead of filling up the whole rectangle. If you want to add an ellipse to your code, copy the following line into line 19:

```
pygame.draw.ellipse(game_screen, white, (300, 200, 40, 80))
```

Save and try running your code to see the red circle, blue rectangle, and white ellipse in the black background:

```
python sample.py
```

If you have written your code without error, you should expect to see something like this:

Experimenting with shapes

Now that you know how to make a circle, rectangle, and ellipse, you can start experimenting with each of the arguments. Changing the radius, width, or height of a shape will change the size. Changing the *x* axis, *y* axis, or both will change the location of the shape on the screen. Here are some experiments to try:

- Change the radius of the circle
- Change the *x* and *y* coordinates of each shape
- Change the width and height of the rectangle and ellipse
- Change the color of each shape

More advanced shapes

There are some more advanced shapes that you can create with pygame, including polygons with as many sides as you like. You can explore the different functions in the `pygame.draw` module by visiting the pygame docs.

 To know more about shapes in pygame, visit
https://www.pygame.org/docs/ref/draw.html.

Making moving objects

Now, video games worth playing have moving objects. Moving objects have a lot more problems to solve than stationary objects. Here are some questions to ask about moving objects:

- Where do you want the object to originate on the screen?
- How does the object *move*?
- How does the object know how fast to move?
- How does the object respond when it hits another object (collides)?
- How does the object respond when it hits the edge of the screen?
- How does the object know when to stop moving?

We create a moving object the same way that we create a stationary one—draw it on the screen.

Moving objects with the keyboard

Let's suppose that we want to move our red circle around the screen. Something we need to consider is that the objects do not actually move. Rather, the objects appear to move. This is how you get an object to move:

- Draw an object
- Get the user's input from pressed keys
- Redraw the object based on user actions using `pygame.display.update()`

The `pygame.key` module contains methods to work with the keyboard. During the game loop, we need to know whether the user is pressing a key to move the blue rectangle. To figure out whether the user is pressing a key to move the rectangle, we would use this line of code, for example:

```
pygame.key.get_pressed()
```

Now, if we want to control how the computer takes the input when a user presses a key, we can use this line of code:

```
pygame.key.set_repeat()
```

This line tells the computer what to do when someone holds the key or presses it repeatedly, which happens a lot in games. We would use these key functions to set up some if/else logic about how our blue rectangles move when certain keys are pressed. You will see this logic in the next chapter.

Now, there are a lot of keys on the keyboard. Before going on to the next chapter, it is a good idea to review the documentation for pygame and learn how to select your keys. For example, if you want to use the down arrow key, you would use `[pygame.K_DOWN]` to identify that key, and then use other code to take a look at what happens if the down key is being pressed.

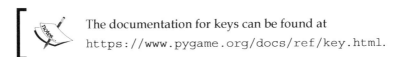

The documentation for keys can be found at
`https://www.pygame.org/docs/ref/key.html`.

A quick task for you

Q1. How do you start pygame?

1. `pygame.display.set_mode()`
2. `pygame.init()`

3. `pygame.exit()`

4. `pygame.quit`

Q2. How do objects move in pygame?

1. Objects move using speed

2. Objects move using gravity

3. Objects move using collision detection

4. Objects only appear to move, but they are actually constantly redrawn.

Q3. How is an object redrawn using pygame?

1. `pygame.rerender()`

2. `pygame.display.object()`

3. `pygame.display.update()`

4. `pygame.rect()`

Q4. What is the shorthand used to identify keys in pygame?

1. pygame.K_keyname

2. pygame.keyname

3. pygame.keys.K.name

4. pygame.key

Summary

In this chapter, you learned about the aspects of pygame that are needed to make an interactive game. You started with finding and installing the software on your operating system. Then, you learned to import and initialize pygame to interact with the computer. You set the characteristics of your game screen, including size and color. You added stationary objects to the game screen and learned some ways to make changes to these objects. You got an explanation of code for moving objects, which we will create in our final game.

In our next chapter, we will build a full-fledged game using all the skills that we have built throughout this book. It is recommended that you through the book again, and repeat any exercises that you do not fully understand. It is highly recommended that you visit the pygame documentation as well and read as much as you are able to understand. There are descriptions and examples of the methods used in this chapter that will help you in the next chapter. Are you ready to put everything together? Let's proceed to *Chapter 9, Tiny Tennis*.

9
Tiny Tennis

In the previous chapter, you learned about the basic modules, classes, and functions in pygame. You learned about these functions so that you can build a new game called **Tiny Tennis**. Tiny Tennis will be a two-player game that uses the keys on a keyboard to control two paddles, which hit a ball back and forth. While this game seems simple when you watch it, there are many different parts needed to make the game playable.

Introduction to game programming principles

There are many principles of game programming that apply to our project in this chapter. First, remember that the movement of objects in space is an illusion that we create. Unlike reality, objects that we create will appear to move because we will regularly draw and then redraw the objects in different places.

Another principle that we have discussed is a game loop. The game loop is important as it controls all of the things that need to happen in the game, including the moving and redrawing of objects. The timing of the game loop is important as this will tell the computer how many times to run the game loop. Each time a game loop runs is also known as a **frame**, and the speed at which the game loop runs is known as the **frame rate**.

Finally, considering how the player interacts with the game is an important part of the game design. This means that we will consider how the player uses keys and has their score stored in the program's memory and displayed somewhere on the screen.

The game plan

Before we start to write any lines of code, we need to have our Python shell, terminal, and text editor open. We will be switching back and forth between these tools as we write and test lines of code throughout the chapter. Set up your monitor so that you are comfortable switching between each window.

Once you set up your workspace, go to the text editor window. We are going to outline our game in the text editor window using comments so that we can better organize our work.

Creating an outline of game parts

We are going to work on this game in four sections. The sections of the game are as follows:

- Section 1: imports, globals, and drawings
- Section 2: moving the paddles
- Section 3: moving the ball
- Section 4: draw screen and track the score

Create a file called `tiny.py` in your text editor. Then, type the following lines into your `tiny.py` file:

```
# imports, globals and drawing


# moving the paddles
# moving the ball
# keeping score
```

Once you are done typing the preceding lines, save your file. This file now provides a general outline of the work that needs to be done to create your game. Here is how your file will look:

```
1 # imports, globals and drawing
2 # moving the paddles
3 # moving the ball
4 # keeping score
```

We are following one particular approach to making this game of Tiny Tennis. It is important to note that there are *MANY* possible ways to write this game code. The way we are doing it here allows us to review all of the concepts that we learned along the way in this book. At the end of this chapter as well as in the next chapter, we will discuss some more advanced (and more streamlined) coding techniques that you can use to make this game do more things and do them more efficiently. Right now, though, let's start this game!

Section 1 – imports, globals, and drawings

In this first section, we will write all of the code to set up the different parts of our game. This includes importing libraries, defining all of our global variables, and telling the computer how to draw the screen, ball, and paddles.

Importing libraries

The first lines of code we write will be used to import the necessary libraries into the game, including pygame. We will be using three libraries in the game: pygame, math, and random. pygame, as we discussed in the previous chapter, allows us to have visual elements in our game. The random library, included with Python, gives us the ability to select and use random numbers in our game. The math library, also included with Python, allows for mathematics with floating point numbers. To use these modules and libraries in your code, type the following lines into your `tiny.py` file underneath the #imports, globals, and drawing comment:

```
import pygame
import random
import time
```

Make sure to save your `tiny.py` file now that you have added some new lines. Be in the habit of saving your code as *OFTEN* as you can.

You can make comments in your code if it helps you to organize your thoughts. Now, we will also initialize pygame so that we are able to use all of the capabilities, including starting our screen, drawing graphics, and running our game loop. To initialize pygame, we use the `init()` function. To initialize it, type these two lines of code below your imports:

```
# initialize pygame
pygame.init()
```

Using `pygame.init()` starts the pygame process, and the pygame process will keep running until the program stops running when the player quits pygame. This allows us to access everything inside of pygame throughout the game. You will see how important this is as we continue to write our game. Right now, save your `tiny.py` file again:

```
1 # imports
2 import pygame
3 import random
4 import time
5
6 # initialize pygame
7 pygame.init()
```

Introducing globals

Now that we have imported the libraries that we need, we will be making globals for some parts of the game. As a reminder, globals, or global variables, are variables that we can use throughout the entire file. We will set global variables for all of the colors that we wish to use. We also set global variables for the screen, paddles, and ball.

Defining a color

First, we will make globals for each color. Colors, as we learned in *Chapter 8, pygame,* are represented by three different numbers listed in parentheses, also called a tuple. Instead of having to write these numbers repeatedly, we will make a global variable for each color so that we can use the names of all of the colors throughout the game.

Depending on what colors you like, you might want to make global variables for all the colors or only for a few. It is really up to you to decide what colors to add to your code. Here is a list of common colors that you may wish to use in your game. You should add the code for each color exactly as it appears here:

```
red = (255, 0, 0)
orange = (255, 127, 0)
yellow = (255, 255, 0)
green: (0, 255, 0)
blue = (0, 0, 255)
violet = (127, 0, 255)
brown = (102, 51, 0)
black = (0, 0, 0)
white = (255, 255, 255)
```

The preceding list shows the basic colors that you can include in your game code. If you want to include more advanced colors, you can search for `rgb color codes chart` in an Internet search engine, such as Google, and you will find that there are different variations for each color that you can change to your liking, such as light blue or dark blue. Once you have changed all the colors to your liking, make sure that you save your work:

```
# imports
import pygame
import random
import time

# initialize pygame
pygame.init()

# color globals
red = (255, 0, 0)
orange = (255, 127, 0)
yellow = (255, 255, 0)
green = (0, 255, 0)
blue = (0, 0, 255)
violet = (127, 0, 255)
brown = (102, 51, 0)
black = (0, 0, 0)
white = (255, 255, 255)
```

Adjusting the screen size

We will also use globals to define the parts of our screen display. This lets us show the size, color, and text for the main screen. Here are the color globals; we will add these lines of code for the width and height of the screen:

```
# screen globals
screen_width = 600
screen_height = 400
```

Now that we have made the `screen_width` and `screen_height` variables, we can use these variables throughout our code, which makes our code easier to read. Also, if we do decide to change the screen width or screen height, we can change it one at a time in this global variable, and all of our code will still run properly.

Drawing the screen

So, the `screen_width` and `screen_height` variables are the basic information that pygame needs so that it can set up the actual game screen. pygame has a function called `pygame.display.set_mode()` that takes the variables of `screen_width` and `screen_height` to make the screen display. Now, writing `pygame.display.set_mode ((screen_width, screen_height))` is really long, especially if we keep doing it. Instead, we are going to set this to a global variable called `game_screen`:

```
game_screen = pygame.display.set_mode((screen_width, screen_height))
```

Creating screen labels

The next set of functions that we use will set the text for the top of the screen and the font for the game screen. The first line of code defines what string of text we want to see, and in the following line, we define the font and size. If the font and the size are not available, the font will, by default, use whatever is originally set on your system. This is true for Windows, Mac, and Linux systems:

```
pygame.display.set_caption("Tiny Tennis")
font = pygame.font.SysFont("monospace", 75)
```

So, we have now set all of the basic variables needed to create a game screen. Save your work and, when you are ready, move on to making the global variables that we will need for the ball, paddles, and scoring. Your screen code should look like this code sample:

```
19
20 # screen globals
21 screen_width = 600
22 screen_height = 400
23 game_screen = pygame.display.set_mode((screen_width, screen_height))
24 pygame.display.set_caption("Tiny Tennis")
25 font = pygame.font.SysFont("monospace", 75)
26
```

Ball – the starting location

In Tiny Tennis, the ball is one of the most important parts of the game. We have a lot to do to make it work. First, we need to give the ball some global characteristics so that it can be drawn and redrawn to create the illusion of movement.

First, we need to set the *x, y* coordinates of the ball. By making a global variable for this, we can tell the computer where to redraw the ball without having to write special code for each movement of the ball. We will set the default value of x and y so that the ball starts in the center of the screen. Write the next lines into your `tiny.py` file:

```
# ball globals
ball_x = int(screen_width / 2)
ball_y = int(screen_height / 2)
```

Ball – setting the speed and direction

Now that we have told the ball to start in the center of the screen as default, we need to tell the ball how far to move by giving it x and y coordinates for movement:

```
ball_xv = 3
ball_yv = 3
```

The `ball_xv = 3` means that the ball will move 3 pixels along the *x* axis each time it is redrawn. The `ball_yv = 3` means that the ball will move 3 pixels along the *y* axis each time the screen redraws. This is great as it will help us keep the ball going in the speed and direction that we like. Here, *v = velocity* which is the magnitude (speed) and direction (*x,y*) of the ball. So, when we say `ball_xv = 3`, we are really saying that *the ball moves along the x axis at a speed of 3 pixels each time the screen is redrawn.*

Ball – setting the size

The final thing that we will define about the ball is its radius. The radius is half of the total width of the ball, as represented in pixels. By setting the radius, we set the size. Write the following line of code into your `tiny.py` file to represent the ball radius:

```
ball_r = 20
```

Now that we have defined the characteristics of the ball, make sure to save the file. Nobody wants to rewrite lines of working code! Take a look at an example of this section of code:

```
26
27 # ball globals
28 ball_x = int(screen_width / 2)
29 ball_y = int(screen_height / 2)
30 ball_xv = 3
31 ball_yv = 3
32 ball_r = 20
33
```

Paddles – starting location and size

In our game, we will have two paddles. Recall that in the beginning of this chapter, it was said that there is more than one way to do some of the things that we are doing. There are more advanced ways to make the paddles, but it is important that you understand each part of the paddle, so we are going to break our code down very simply. Later, once you have completed this game, you can do some research on creating objects and try creating paddles as objects.

We will give our paddle four qualities: a starting location on the *x* axis, a starting location on the *y* axis, a width, and a height. Each of these numbers is a representation in pixels. Below the ball globals, on line 34, add the next five lines to your `tiny.py` file:

```
# draw paddle 1
paddle1_x = 10
paddle1_y = 10
paddle1_w = 25
paddle1_h = 100
```

You probably noticed that the code we wrote is for `paddle1`. There are two paddles required for Tiny Tennis. We want to give each player a fair start, so we will create `paddle2` so that it is equal in size, but it's located opposite `paddle1`. To make the second paddle, start on line 40 and write the next five lines of code:

```
# draw paddle 2
paddle2_x = screen_width - 35
paddle2_y = 10
paddle2_w = 25
paddle2_h = 100
```

You will notice that the x coordinate for paddle 2 combines `the screen_width` variable, which is the maximum x coordinate number (`600`) and then subtracts the width of the paddle (`25`) + the x coordinate value of paddle 1 (`10`) as well. This math allows us to make sure that the paddle is the same distance from the right-hand side of the screen as it is from the left-hand side of the screen. If you are confused, copy the code into your file and save it. You can play with the numbers and see how your paddles change based on each value:

```
33
34 # draw paddle 1
35 paddle1_x = 10
36 paddle1_y = 10
37 paddle1_w = 25
38 paddle1_h = 100
39
40 # draw paddle 2
41 paddle2_x = screen_width - 35
42 paddle2_y = 10
43 paddle2_w = 25
44 paddle2_h = 100
45
```

Initializing the score

In order to have a score, we are going to create a variable for each player that begins at the default score, zero. As this is a global variable, like the other integers, it will change as the game loop runs. For now, we just need to have placeholders for each player. So, starting on line 46, add these lines of code to your game:

```
# initialize score
player1_score = 0
player2_score = 0
```

We have now created all of the global variables that we need to write code that is easier to understand. Remember, these are called global variables because they can be used throughout the entire code file. Save your file. Then, compare your code with the completed code in this screenshot:

```
 9  # color globals
10  red = (255, 0, 0)
11  orange = (255, 127, 0)
12  yellow = (255, 255, 0)
13  green = (0, 255, 0)
14  blue = (0, 0, 255)
15  violet = (127, 0, 255)
16  brown = (102, 51, 0)
17  black = (0, 0, 0)
18  white = (255, 255, 255)
19
20  # screen globals
21  screen_width = 600
22  screen_height = 400
23  game_screen = pygame.display.set_mode((screen_width, screen_height))
24  pygame.display.set_caption("Tiny Tennis")
25  font = pygame.font.SysFont("monospace", 75)
26
27  # ball globals
28  ball_x = int(screen_width / 2)
29  ball_y = int(screen_height / 2)
30  ball_xv = 3
31  ball_yv = 3
32  ball_r = 20
33
34  # paddles
35  paddle1_x = 10
36  paddle1_y = 10
37  paddle1_w = 25
38  paddle1_h = 100
39
40  # Due to x position determined at upper left, we combine width of paddle and paddle1_x to achieve same distance
41  paddle2_x = screen_width - 35
42  paddle2_y = 10
43  paddle2_w = 25
44  paddle2_h = 100
45
46  # score
47  player1_score = 0
48  player2_score = 0
49
```

Testing section 1

Now that we have imported libraries, initialized pygame, and created globals for colors, the screen, ball, and the paddles, we can run our first tests to check how things are going. To test the game, you will need to locate the directory where you saved your `tiny.py` file in your terminal/command prompt. In earlier games, we made this directory on the desktop. Once you navigate to the directory where `tiny.py` is saved, you can run the following commands from the terminal/command prompt to see your game so far:

```
python tiny.py
```

When you run this command, you should see a window pop up and then close. The window will not stay open because we have not written any of the code that runs the game; however, if the code runs and there are *NO ERRORS* in your terminal/command prompt, then you can keep moving forward with confidence.

If there are errors in your code, now is a good time to fix them. Some common errors that can take place include syntax errors (using the wrong symbols), typos (spelling something incorrectly, such as a Python keyword), or trying to run your file from the wrong directory. If you have errors, check for these common errors, and fix the mistakes in your code.

If you get an error that is not one of the aforementioned common errors, you can always perform an Internet search to ask a question about the problem you are having. It is very common for even experienced developers to use Internet searches to find help to fix errors, and there are many websites and blogs that people maintain in order to help others learn.

Section 2 – moving the paddles

Now we finally get to write the code that will make our paddles appear on the screen and allow us to control the paddle.

This is where we get the chance to use the logic and loops that we learned about in earlier chapters. In a game such as Tiny Tennis, many decisions are made very quickly. Computers are great at making fast decisions based on our instructions. Here are the parts of the code that will be in the next section:

- Creating the `while` loop
- Key events

We will code these next pieces step by step, and then test the code by running it to check whether there are any errors. It is suggested that you read through this whole section before you start coding so that you know what to expect. Once you have read through everything, the fun starts!

Pre-loop actions

Before we actually create the `while` loop, there are two actions that we will code. The first is to ensure that the cursor disappears when it goes over the game screen, so it is not an interruption. There is a special function for this behavior in pygame:

```
pygame.mouse.set_visible(0)
```

By setting the visibility to 0, we make the mouse/cursor invisible to the game. Since we do not need the mouse in the game, it is okay for us to do this.

The second action is to set the global variable for our `while` loop. We are going to call our main game loop variable `do_main`. We will set `do_main = True`:

```
do_main = True
```

> Remember that syntax and case (uppercase or lowercase) are important. Notice the *CAPITAL* letter *T*, and make sure to copy it exactly as it is. Remember, *True* is a Boolean that needs to be written with a capital *T*. Now, we are ready to write our `while` loop.

Creating the while loop

Our game loop will be a `while` loop. We will use `do_main` as our `True` statement. So, you will have another line of code that looks like this:

```
while do_main:
```

Make sure you place a colon (:) at the end of the line. Also, all of the other lines of code in the game loop will be indented at least once because they all need to be *INSIDE* of the loop to run. Here is a screenshot of the `while` loop:

```
50  # game loop
51  pygame.mouse.set_visible(0)    # makes mouse invisible in game screen
52  do_main = True
53  while do_main:
54      pressed = pygame.key.get_pressed()
55      pygame.key.set_repeat
56      for event in pygame.event.get():
57          if event.type == pygame.QUIT:
58              do_main = False
59
60      if pressed[pygame.K_ESCAPE]:
61          do_main = False
62
63      if pressed[pygame.K_w]:
64          paddle1_y -= 5
65      elif pressed[pygame.K_s]:
66          paddle1_y += 5
67
68      if pressed[pygame.K_UP]:
69          paddle2_y -= 5
70      elif pressed[pygame.K_DOWN]:
71          paddle2_y += 5
72
```

Moving the paddles – keyboard events

The first set of events in the `while` loop are keyboard events. These events take place when a key or set of keys get pressed. The events use the `if/elif` logic. All of them are indented on at least one tab, and some are indented on two tabs or more. Remember that indents are an organizational tool in Python and help us keep track of when certain code should be run.

Notice the code on line 54 of the screenshot. In line 54, we will create the pressed variable, which we will set equal to the `pygame.key.get_pressed()` function. This will give us a shorter reference to the function. Type this code in line 54:

```
pressed = pygame.key.get_pressed()
```

In line 55, we use the `pygame.key.set_repeat()` function. This tells the computer that once a key is pressed, the action that the key performs should continue until the user lets the key go. Type the next line of code into line 55 of your `tiny.py` file:

```
pygame.key.set_repeat()
```

Now that we have set the variable and characteristics for the keyboard events, we will create our first loop, a `for` loop that looks for the player to quit. Using a `for` loop, we will loop over each event that is found using the `pygame.event.get()` function. If the event is a *QUIT* event, then the `while` loop will automatically end. You will notice that we also use our `if` logic here so that we can tell the computer to make a decision if it finds the quit event. To make this `for` loop, you will write the following lines of code, starting on line 56 of your code file:

```
for event in pygame.event.get():
  if event.type == pygame.QUIT:
    do_main = False
```

Now that we have told the computer how and when to end the `while` loop, we can tell the computer what to do when certain keys are pressed. For our Tiny Tennis game, we need to assign keys to exit the game as well as ones to control paddle 1 and paddle 2.

 Want to choose different keys than the ones we use in this book? You can find an entire list of how to use every keyboard key on the pygame website at http://www.pygame.org/docs/ref/key.html.

Exiting the game – escape key

To exit the game, we will use the *Esc* key. You will notice that we use our pressed variable followed by the key code for the *Esc* key. Starting from line 60, type these two lines of code:

```
if pressed[pygame.K_ESCAPE]:
    do_main = False
```

The lines of code tell the computer that if the *Esc* key is pressed, then the do_main global variable should be set to False. When do_main is set to Boolean False, then the while loop stops. We will write the code that ends the game a bit later.

Paddle control – player 1

For player 1's paddle to go up, we will use the *W* key. For player 1's paddle to go down, we will use the *S* key. These are very typical keys to use for computer game controls. Notice which letters are uppercase and which are lowercase, and be sure to copy them exactly, starting from line 63:

```
if pressed[pygame.K_w]:
    paddle1_y -= 5
elif pressed[pygame.K_s]:
    paddle1_y += 5
```

Paddle control – player 2

Player 2 also needs to have keyboard controls that work to move his/her paddle up and down at the same time as player 1. This means that we must assign different keys for the second paddle. For this game, we are using the up arrow key to move paddle 2 up and the down arrow key to move paddle 2 down. Type the following lines of code into your tiny.py file, starting from line 68:

```
if pressed[pygame.K_UP]:
    paddle2_y -= 5
elif pressed[pygame.K_DOWN]:
    paddle2_y += 5
```

 Save your work!

The increase and decrease value (-= and +=)

You will notice the -= and += symbols in this code. These symbols are used as shortcuts to increase or decrease the value of something. In the code for moving the paddles, we use these symbols to add or subtract values when the paddle keys are pressed. Both the -= and += symbols are very important for setting the proper paddle position each time the paddles are moved by the user.

Testing section 2

Time to test our code again. In your terminal/command prompt, locate the directory where you saved your `tiny.py` file. In earlier games, we made this directory on the desktop. Once you navigate to the directory where `tiny.py` is saved, you can run the following command from the terminal/command prompt to see your game so far:

```
python tiny.py
```

During this test, you will see a window open that says **Tiny Tennis** at the top and is totally blank otherwise. See this screenshot:

If you are getting errors, remember to check your code for typos, syntax errors, and case errors.

Section 3 – moving the ball

Now that we have written and tested the code for the paddles, we need to write code to move the ball. We will be changing the location of the ball with some of our code, and we will create something called collision detection.

Moving the ball – updating the location

First, we need to be constantly calculating the x and y coordinates of the ball based on the velocity of the ball that we set in the global variables. This allows us to make constant updates as long as we are playing the game. To make sure that the x and y coordinates of the ball update as the ball moves, you will type the following lines of code, starting from line 74:

```
# location of ball is updated
ball_x += ball_xv
ball_y += ball_yv
```

Collision detection

Our next job is to code something called **collision detection**. This means that we can program the computer to know when two objects are hitting one another. We can also tell the computer what we want it to do when the objects collide. In Tiny Tennis, we have three kinds of collisions that we want to detect:

- Collision of the ball with the top and bottom of the screen
- Collision of the paddle with the top and bottom of the screen
- Collision of the ball with the paddle

Collision of the ball with the top and the bottom of the screen

Next, we will use our `if` statement to define what happens if the ball hits the top or the bottom of the screen. Basically, we want the ball to bounce back if it hits the top or bottom of the screen. Type the following code starting from line 77 of your `tiny.py` file:

```
# collision of ball with top/bottom of screen
if ball_y - ball_r <= 0 or ball_y + ball_r >= screen_height:
    ball_yv *= -1
```

The first line, beginning with `if`, basically says *If the radius is subtracted from the y coordinate and that is less than or equal to zero OR if the radius is added to the y coordinate and it is greater than the number of the screen height (400), then do something about it.*

The second line of the code that comes after the colon tells us what to do: *the velocity of the y coordinate of the ball should be in the reverse direction.* The second line of code, `ball_yv *= -1`, means that the velocity of the y coordinate gets reversed because it is multiplied by `-1`. Any number multiplied by `-1` becomes opposite to its original sign, and, in this case, reversing the sign means reversing the direction of the ball.

So, why does this code work? Let's think about it. The top y coordinate is zero. If the ball tries to move past the top, its y value will be less than zero, which means that it will be out of the screen. To make the ball stay on the screen, we change its direction when the y coordinate value is less than zero.

The bottom y coordinate is `400`. So, if the ball's y value is greater than `400`, then we change the direction of the ball to go back up. We make these directional changes by multiplying the velocity of the ball by `-1`, resulting in a directional change.

Before moving on, compare your code to this code:

```
76
77    # collision of ball with top/bottom of screen
78    if ball_y - ball_r <= 0 or ball_y + ball_r >= screen_height:
79        ball_yv *= -1
80
81    # collision of paddle with edges of screen
82    if paddle1_y < 0:
83        paddle1_y = 0
84    elif paddle1_y + paddle1_h > screen_height:
85        paddle1_y = screen_height - paddle1_h
86
```

Collision of the paddle with the top and the bottom of screen

We want the paddle to stop when it reaches the top or bottom of the screen. To make this happen, we need to create a code that will recognize the y value of the paddle and then stop the paddle from moving beyond the two y values that create the screen borders. These two values are `0` for the top of the screen, and `400` for the bottom. Copy the following lines of code into your program, starting from line 81. Check to make sure that your indent level is correct:

```
# collision of paddle with top/bottom of screen
if paddle1_y < 0:
    paddle1_y = 0
```

```
    elif paddle1_y + paddle1_h > screen_height:
        paddle1_y = screen_height - paddle1_h


    if paddle2_y < 0:
        paddle2_y = 0
    elif paddle2_y + paddle2_h > screen_height:
        paddle2_y = screen_height - paddle2_h
```

This code works differently from the ball code because we do not want the paddles to bounce around! Instead, we want the paddles to stop when they hit the top or bottom of the screen. So, you will notice that whenever paddle 1 or paddle 2 goes beyond the barriers of the screen (0 and 400), the value of the paddle is reset to *EQUAL* the boundary values of 0 or 400, depending on *WHERE* the paddle is located (is it at the top of the screen or the bottom?). Save your work once you are done with adding this code.

Collision of the ball with the paddles

The collision of the ball with the paddles will determine what happens when the ball hits the paddle. There are two paddles, and it will be helpful if you add some comment code using a hashtag to keep track of the code for the left-hand side paddle (paddle 1) and the right-hand side paddle (paddle 2).

Now that we have done some collision detection, let's think about the ball and paddle. When the ball hits the paddle, we want the ball to appear as though it has bounced off of the paddle. Therefore, we need to make sure that the result of the collision between the ball and the paddle is that the ball reverses itself and goes in the opposite direction. This is actually the same behavior that we used to make the ball bounce off the edges of the screen, except now we need to outline all the pieces of paddle 1 and paddle 2. Copy these lines of code into your file:

```
    # left paddle
    if ball_x < paddle1_x + paddle1_w and ball_y >= paddle1_y and ball_y
<= paddle1_y + paddle1_h:
        ball_xv *= -1
    # right paddle
    if ball_x > paddle2_x and ball_y >= paddle2_y and ball_y <= paddle2_y
+ paddle2_h:
        ball_xv *= -1
```

Take a look at this screenshot, and compare your code:

```
72
73    # velocity of ball is set
74    ball_x += ball_xv
75    ball_y += ball_yv
76
77    # collision of ball with edges of screen
78    if ball_y - ball_r <= 0 or ball_y + ball_r >= screen_height:
79        ball_yv *= -1
80
81    # collision of paddle with edges of screen
82    if paddle1_y < 0:
83        paddle1_y = 0
84    elif paddle1_y + paddle1_h > screen_height:
85        paddle1_y = screen_height - paddle1_h
86
87    if paddle2_y < 0:
88        paddle2_y = 0
89    elif paddle2_y + paddle2_h > screen_height:
90        paddle2_y = screen_height - paddle2_h
91
92    # collision of ball and paddles
93    # left paddle
94    if ball_x < paddle1_x + paddle1_w and ball_y >= paddle1_y and ball_y <= paddle1_y + paddle1_h:
95        ball_xv *= -1
96    # right paddle
97    if ball_x > paddle2_x and ball_y >= paddle2_y and ball_y <= paddle2_y + paddle2_h:
98        ball_xv *= -1
```

Testing – section 3

You are almost done writing the game! Now it's time to test our code again. In your terminal/command prompt, locate the directory where you saved your `tiny.py` file. You can run the following command from the terminal/command prompt to check the progress of your game so far:

```
python tiny.py
```

During this test, if everything is working correctly, your results will be the same as the test from Section 2. A blank screen will open and will be called Tiny Tennis. Congratulations!

If your program has some errors while running, look at the error messages to check whether you can figure out what is going wrong. Look for syntax mistakes, spelling mistakes, indentation mistakes, or any other errors in your code. Make sure that you are using spaces for your indentations, not tabs, or else you might have problems as well.

Section 4 – draw screen and track the score

So, we know that the ball bounces off the top and bottom of the screen as well as off the paddles. However, if the user misses the ball with the paddle, what happens to the ball? What happens to the player and their score?

In this section of the game, we use the location of the x coordinates to determine whether the ball is on the screen or it has gone past the paddles and is outside the screen. We use our `if` statement to tell the computer what to do. The *x* axis 0 coordinate is the left-most side of the screen. If the ball's x value is less than 0, then the player on the other side (player 2) has scored a point because player 1 failed to block the ball. If you read the lines of code, you will notice that we reset the `ball_x` and `ball_y` coordinates to the center of the screen so that a new game can start. Copy the next four lines of code to place this logic into the game:

```
if ball_x <= 0:
    player2_score += 1
    ball_x = int(screen_width / 2)
    ball_y = int(screen_height / 2)
```

You will notice that the next four lines of code are almost identical, with only two changes. The ball's x value is now being compared to the maximum screen width, which is 600. If the ball's x value becomes greater than 600, it means that the player has missed the ball and the ball is now outside of the screen. Now, player 1 has scored because player 2 did not block the ball. To make sure that this logic is also in the game, copy the next four lines of code into your file:

```
elif ball_x >= screen_width:
    player1_score += 1
    ball_x = int(screen_width / 2)
    ball_y = int(screen_height / 2)
```

```
 99
100    # player score
101    if ball_x <= 0:
102        player2_score += 1
103        ball_x = int(screen_width / 2)
104        ball_y = int(screen_height / 2)
105    elif ball_x >= screen_width:
106        player1_score += 1
107        ball_x = int(screen_width / 2)
108        ball_y = int(screen_height / 2)
109
```

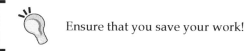 Ensure that you save your work!

The render screen – show what's happened

The final code that we need to write is the code that redraws the screen and all of the objects so that the movements appear to happen. The next lines of code draw the five objects that are a part of our game. There is no need to use variable names to draw the paddles, net, or the balls, except that it does make them easier to find if you want to fix or change that part of the code. Again, these lines of code are indented so that they are inside of the `while` loop:

```
game_screen.fill(black)
paddle_1 = pygame.draw.rect(game_screen, white, (paddle1_x, paddle1_y, paddle1_w, paddle1_h), 0)
paddle_2 = pygame.draw.rect(game_screen, white, (paddle2_x, paddle2_y, paddle2_w, paddle2_h), 0)
net = pygame.draw.line(game_screen, yellow, (300,5), (300,400))
ball = pygame.draw.circle(game_screen, red, (ball_x, ball_y), ball_r, 0)
```

The `game_screen.fill(black)` code uses our `game_screen` variable and tells the `fill()` function to make our screen black by putting the color `black` in parentheses. Did you notice that we used two global variables, `game_screen` and `black`, in this line of code? Imagine how much longer the code would be without these variables. Imagine that it might be more difficult to read and to change.

You will notice that the `pygame.draw.rect()` function is used to draw the paddles, since they are just rectangles. The paddles have the following characteristics:

- Game screen (tells you where they should go)
- Color
- An x coordinate
- A y coordinate (to provide a starting location)
- A width
- A height

If you look at the `line()` and `circle()` objects, you will notice that they are not too different from the rectangle. Both have a `game_screen` and color property. The line object accepts arguments that define a length, width, and *x* value for the line. The circle object accepts arguments that define `game_screen`, color, and ball characteristics. Since we defined the ball characteristics early in the chapter with global variables, we can use them in the `circle()` code.

Displaying player scores

Our next few lines of code will draw the player scores on the screen:

```
    score_text = font.render(str(player1_score) + " " + str(player2_
score), 1, white)
    game_screen.blit(score_text, (screen_width / 2 - score_text.get_
width() / 2, 10))
```

The top line of our game score code provides the definition for the `score_text` variable, which is used in the second line of this code that we just added. The `game_screen.blit()` function copies our score text each time our screen is redrawn, since the score text may not change for a long time if neither player misses the ball.

Finally, the `pygame.display.update()` function updates the image with the new information stored by our program. Because a computer can move at speeds infinitely faster than a human, we have added a `sleep` option, allowing for the update to occur at an interval that we can now control:

```
pygame.display.update()
time.sleep(0.016666667)
```

Ending the program

The final line of code will be to end the initialization of pygame, which we performed at the start of the code. To end this, we will type `pygame.quit()` at the outermost level of indentation in our code. This goes outside of the `while` loop so that it only happens when the `while` loop stops running:

```
pygame.quit()
```

Once you have typed this, your final game code lines should look like this:

```
109
110     game_screen.fill(black)
111     paddle_1 = pygame.draw.rect(game_screen, white, (paddle1_x, paddle1_y, paddle1_w, paddle1_h), 0)
112     paddle_2 = pygame.draw.rect(game_screen, white, (paddle2_x, paddle2_y, paddle2_w, paddle2_h), 0)
113     net = pygame.draw.line(game_screen, yellow, (300,5), (300,400))
114     ball = pygame.draw.circle(game_screen, red, (ball_x, ball_y), ball_r, 0)
115
116     score_text = font.render(str(player1_score) + " " + str(player2_score), 1, white)
117     game_screen.blit(score_text, (screen_width / 2 - score_text.get_width() / 2, 10))
118
119     pygame.display.update()
120
121     time.sleep(0.016666667)
122
123 pygame.quit()
124 # game end
```

Once you have double-checked your code against the screenshots in the chapter, make sure that you save your `tiny.py` file. Now you are ready to truly give your game a test!

Play Tiny Tennis!

The best part about Tiny Tennis is that you can play it against yourself, making it easy to test the game and experiment with different parts of the game. Now, when you run the file from your terminal, a window that looks like this should pop up:

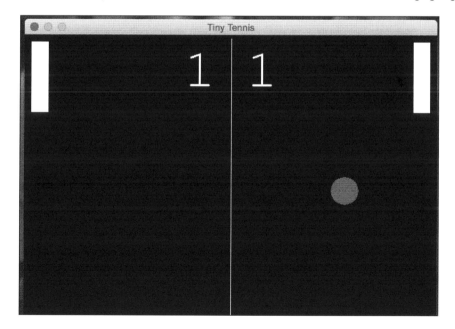

The ball should start moving immediately toward one side or the other of the screen. You can test the game by making sure that the paddles on each side of the screen are able to hit the ball and that they do not go outside of the screen space. You can test the scoring mechanism to make sure that the appropriate player is getting the points for each shot that they make past the other player. Then, you can invite others to play the game with you.

If you are not happy with parts of the game, you can change them. For example, you might choose a different color for the ball, paddles, and the screen. Maybe you want the paddles to be longer or shorter or, perhaps, thinner. Maybe you want to make the ball bigger or smaller by changing the radius.

You might decide that you want the ball and paddles to move faster so that the game is more challenging, or maybe you want the ball and paddles to move slower if you are designing the game to be played by younger children. Design choices are made for many reasons, and now that you have a playable game, you might decide to make some different design decisions.

You can test your decisions by making a copy of your game code and then testing any modifications in your copy. It is a good idea to keep a backup of your working code so that if you write broken code, you have a place to return to and start again.

Summary

Congratulations on building your first game! There are so many things that you learned to do. The greatest thing about code, though, is that there are many ways to do everything. Some ways are easier to understand but not as efficient as other ways. Some code is very efficient but might not be easily understood by another programmer. The best code is both easy to understand and written in the most efficient way possible.

Throughout the previous chapter, we used a combination of code that was easy to understand, but may not have been as efficient as possible. This is because we were learning many new principles in pygame, and things, such as collision detection, can be challenging to code. You may decide to do things differently after you have a few games under your belt!

In the next chapter, we will review all that we have learned in this book, and we will also take a look at some other ways that Python is used out in the world, as Python is a very useful language to know. See you in the last chapter!

10
Keep Coding!

In the previous chapter, we built a complete two-player game in a graphical environment using pygame. In the final chapter of this book, we will review all that you learned from the beginning of this journey, and then explore some other ideas that you can try with your new coding skills. Many of these ideas will be games, but some ideas will involve other ways in which Python can be used.

What we learned and your next steps

At the beginning of this book, you started out by learning about your computer. You learned how to install Python and use different free tools such as text editors, the Python shell, and a terminal/command line to run your games. Also, you learned how to navigate to your desktop directory and save your work so that you could work through each project. The next steps included the following:

- Navigating to other folders and directories on your computer
- Learning more terminal/command prompt commands

We then started our coding journey by making functions and variables, and using different data types. We created some functions to do mathematics, and then we put those functions together to create a calculator. You learned how to get information from someone by giving them a prompt using the `input()` command.

We used logic such as `if` and `else` to teach the computer how to make decisions based on what the user decided to do. We also used loops to help us perform different jobs in games. The steps after this would include the following:

- Looking up and trying to understand nested `if` statements
- Using loops to work with large text or datasets

You learned about the different ways to use and store data in Python, such as dictionaries and lists. It is helpful to know how things are stored in Python, and one of the fastest features of Python is its capacity to store and retrieve data very quickly.

Throughout *Chapter 1, Welcome! Let's Get Started*, and *Chapter 9, Tiny Tennis*, we built several projects to show how you could use the skills that you learned. It is important to understand how to use the great features of Python to solve problems. Knowing about each tool means that you can better imagine how to solve a problem using your coding skills. For the remainder of the chapter, let's take a look at some of the problems we can solve that will expand our Python skills.

Classes and objects – very important next steps!

Immediately, you will need to start learning about classes and objects. These are great ways to simplify what would otherwise be repeated code. For example, there is a class in pygame called `Sprites`. The `pygame.Sprites` module has classes that make it easier to manage different game objects.

To learn more about Sprites, it is best to refer to the documentation: `http://www.pygame.org/docs/tut/SpriteIntro.html`.

To learn more about classes and objects, it is a good idea to search the Internet for things such as object-oriented programming (this is the kind of programming that Python uses) and, more specifically, classes and objects. If you find classes and objects confusing, do not worry. This is a concept that takes some getting used to.

Here are some resources that will help you learn about classes and objects:
`http://www.tutorialspoint.com/python/python_classes_objects.htm`
`http://www.learnpython.org/en/Classes_and_Objects`

More fun with games

Since the focus of this book was making game projects, we shall take a look at some more complicated things that you can do with games once you explore pygame in more detail. You can start by making Tiny Tennis more complicated in these ways:

- Adding a music file
- Adding graphics

Adding music to games

pygame allows you to add music to your games. There is a music module that allows you to add music in a few formats to your game files. There are some limitations, including file types. For example, using universally supported `.ogg` file types is better than using file types such as `.mp3`, which are not natively supported on all operating systems.

 For more information, you can go to the pygame site at `https://www.pygame.org/docs/ref/music.html` and learn how to add your favorite sounds.

Adding graphics to games

While you learned how to make some basic shapes, our world would be pretty boring if it only had rectangles, circles, and squares in basic colors. By experimenting with modules such as the `pygame.image()` module you can learn how to work with images that are created outside of pygame. If you have an artistic sibling or friend or you are an artist yourself, you can create or scan artwork in your computer and then add it to your games.

 You can learn about the `pygame.image()` module at `http://www.pygame.org/docs/ref/image.html`.

Remake or design games

If you want a brand new challenge, you can try remaking a classic game on your own. There are a lot of classic games, such as PacMan, Asteroids, or Legend of Zelda. A good challenge would be to try and remake a version of these games using your skills. This practice exercise would require you to do some of these important things:

- Plan your program ahead of time
- Figure out if you need classes in your program
- Figure out how to use objects in your program
- Manage loops in your program
- Manage if/else decisions in your program
- Manage user information, such as the name and score, in your program

Once you make a few games that are based on classic games, you might have some ideas for your own games. If you do have ideas, make notes of them in a file on your computer. When you think about a new game, you need to do the same things that you do to recreate a classic game, except that you need to make other decisions about the purpose of the game, the win conditions of the game, and the controllers.

Other games

Many programmers have made small games in Python to practice their programming skills. To start with, you can look at some other games that people have made and posted on the pygame website. Navigate to http://pygame.org/tags/pygame, and view some of the contributions people have made.

PB-Ball

PB-Ball is a basketball game that uses pygame and adds classes and objects. When you navigate to the project page, you will see a few different links to the code. The following links will help you find the game and look at the code. When you look at the code, you will notice that there are folders for images and sounds. So, there are many new skills to learn in order to create a game that has a more complicated background. Here is a screenshot along with some links to the game so that you can look at the code and learn it:

Here's the link to the PB-Ball game:

`http://pygame.org/project-PB-Ball-2963-.html`

Here is a link to the main code, including two classes and source:

`https://bitbucket.org/tjohnson2/pb-ball/src/8`
`8e324263a63eb97d6a2427f7ea719df85010dfe/main.`
`py?fileviewer=file-view-default`

Here are some files that include images and sounds needed to play the game:

`https://bitbucket.org/tjohnson2/pb-ball/src`

Snake

A game that many people have played is the snake game, where the player starts as a short snake that becomes longer as the game goes on. The only rule to stay alive is that the snake cannot touch its tail. There are many samples of this game available on the Internet. You can view a few samples of code and check whether you are able to recreate the game.

Learn more about the Snake games from the following links:

`http://programarcadegames.com/python_examples/f.`
`php?file=snake.py`

`https://github.com/YesIndeed/SnakesForPython`

`https://github.com/xtur/SnakesAllAround` (this is multiplayer!)

Apart from the preceding games, there are a few programmers who have worked really hard to make Python game instructions available to new programmers! A few such books are available for free on the Internet. Refer to:

Rapid Game Development with Python by Richard Jones (`http://richard.`
`cgpublisher.com/product/pub.84/prod.11`).

Other uses of Python

Python has many uses outside of making games. Learning Python can open doors to careers in data science, web application development, or software testing, among other things. If you really want to make a career in computer programming, then it is a great idea to check out some of the different things you can do with Python.

Curious about how Python is used in the real world? Learn about how Python is used in many different fields! Visit `https://www.python.org/about/success/` for more details.

SciPy

The **SciPy** library has a suite of several programs that are open source (free) and can be used for mathematics, science, and data analysis. Two of those programs will be reviewed here. Although some of the programs are rather advanced in their abilities, they can be used to do simple things. The suite of programs is worth knowing if you want to use Python in work related to your math or science.

Learn about all the programs at `http://www.scipy.org/`.

iPython

iPython is a program that is similar to the Python shells that we used for our projects, including **IDLE** or in the terminal. However, iPython has a server that uses *notebooks* to keep track of your code as well as other notes that you make along with your code. The project is undergoing some positive changes.

Learn about iPython notebook at `http://ipython.org/`.

Packt Publishing offers an introductory book called *Learning IPython for Interactive Computing and Data Visualization* (2015) by Cyrille Rossant to help you learn how to use iPython:

`https://www.packtpub.com/big-data-and-business-intelligence/learning-ipython-interactive-computing-and-data-visualization`.

MatPlotLib

MatPlotLib is an advanced tool that can be coded using Python to create simple or complex charts, graphs, histograms, and even animations. It is an open source project, so it is also free to use. There are many ways to use this tool, which is especially useful for any 2D visualizations. All of the instructions for its download and installation are on its website. There are a lot of dependencies, but if you are keen on mathematics or 2D graphical representations (or both), then you should check out the website and code samples.

Raspberry Pi

The popular Raspberry Pi is a small computer board designed for experimentation in computing and robotics. Its operating system, which is different from Windows and Mac, comes preinstalled with Python and pygame, so it is a very convenient way to get started with gaming since you do not have to do all the work that we did in the first chapter.

To use Raspberry Pi, you will need a power source, a monitor that has an HDMI input, an HDMI cable, a keyboard and mouse, and a Wi-Fi dongle or Ethernet cable if you plan to use the Internet. Additionally, you will need an SD card to install the latest Raspberry Pi operating system. With these items, you can use Raspberry Pi as your primary computer and experiment, knowing that if you crash your computer, you can just make another copy of the operating system for free!

Many people have used Raspberry Pi to make games and even small, handheld game systems! Aside from making games, people have used Raspberry Pi to make robotics projects and media center projects. Something that's very neat about Raspberry Pi is that you can learn more about building computers, and you can try making computers for different uses. You can use Python and Raspberry Pi to write code that controls light switches, door buzzers, and even household appliances! You can visit the official Raspberry Pi website to learn more about its hardware and its Linux-based operating system.

Visit `https://www.raspberrypi.org/` and read *Learning Raspberry Pi* by Samarth Shah (*Packt Publishing*, 2015) and *Raspberry Pi Cookbook for Python Programmers* by Tim Cox (*Packt Publishing*, April 2014) for more details about Raspberry Pi.

Coding challenges

Aside from all of the neat things that you can do with Python code, you can practice coding Python by finding coding challenges and completing them alone or with friends. These challenges range from being short to long, easy to difficult, and are a great way to keep your skills sharp between projects. The coding challenges usually aim at one specific coding skill each, as follows:

- Printing
- Iterating over loops
- Creating variables, strings, and integers
- Data management
- Functions
- `if/elif/else`
- Nested `if/elif/else`
- Nested logic
- Recursing

If you don't feel totally comfortable with these terms, look them up, read more about them, and try some of the coding challenges to strengthen your skills. Here are some websites that have coding challenges in Python:

- `http://codingbat.com/python`
- `http://www.pythonchallenge.com/`
- `http://usingpython.com/python-programming-challenges/`
- `https://wiki.python.org/moin/ProblemSets`
- `https://www.hackerrank.com/login`

You can find hundreds of practice problems in these links!

Summary

Hopefully, this book has provided you a solid introduction to basic Python concepts. By no means are you an expert as Python is a powerful language that can do a lot more than can be presented in one book. However, if you worked through each of the games, you will have a solid Python foundation on which to build your next steps.

One way to keep using Python is to continue to work on challenges and games while digging into code architecture, classes and objects, and more advanced game coding using objects, custom images, sounds, and other effects. Python is not used in traditional game systems, but game design concepts work well in any object-oriented language. Once you are comfortable in Python, you can move toward more common game design languages, such as C++, with a lot more ease.

Another way to use Python is to learn more about data applications and how to use Python to work with different kinds of data and mathematics. This is a really great way to get further into exploring Python and also create a portfolio of work to show upper schools or even colleges. The Internet has large datasets about a variety of topics, including population and weather, among other things.

Finally, you may decide that you want to learn about web applications that are built using Python. If you choose to do so, you can look at places such as GitHub or Bitbucket where programmers keep their code and sometimes allow it to be available for free. Reading the code of other programmers is a fantastic way to learn new and interesting ways to use code. Also, finding and helping build free programs, also called open source, is a great way to help the community get better at programming. You can ask great questions and get answers to them, too.

All the best in your quest to write better games and better code. Keep learning!

Quick Task Answers

This appendix contains answers to all the quick task questions that appear at the end of the chapters. Now, let's have a look at the answers to respective questions.

Chapter 1, Welcome! Let's Get Started

Questions	Answers
Q1. What is a terminal (Mac/Linux) or command prompt (Windows)?	A terminal can do all of the above.
Q2. When you first open the terminal/ command prompt, what do you need to do so that you can start reading and writing the Python code?	Type the word `python`.
Q3. How is the Python shell different from the command line?	The Python shell is started by typing the word `python` into the command line.

Chapter 2, Variables, Functions, and Users

Questions	Answers
Q1. What must a function begin with?	def
Q2. What are conventions that are used to name variables and functions?	All of the above
Q3. Every line after the first line of a function must be?	Indented

Questions	Answers
Q4. If you want a code file to run in Python, you need to end it with?	.py
Q5. To run a code file in the terminal, what do you need to do?	In the correct folder, type `python` and the name of the file

Chapter 3, Calculate This!

Questions	Answers
Q1. What kind of data does the `input()` function return?	Strings
Q2. What does the `int()` function do?	Changes data to whole numbers
Q3. How is the `float()` function different from the `int()` function?	The `float()` function converts data into floating point numbers only
Q4. If you make a function called addition() in your Python shell, how do you run that addition function to test it?	Type `addition()` into your Python shell

Chapter 4, Making Decisions – Python Control Flows

Questions	Answers
Q1. How many times can the `elif` statement appear in the `if/elif/else` flow?	As many times as it is needed
Q2. Which statement starts a conditional block of code that is used to make decisions?	if
Q3. Which statement is only used at the end of a conditional block of code?	else
Q4. What is a global variable?	Both 2 and 3
Q5. What is a `while` loop?	A loop that repeats code until something different happens, and then it stops

Chapter 5, Loops and Logic

Questions	Answers
Q1. What is a Boolean?	A statement that is either `True` or `False`
Q2. Why are global variables helpful?	Choice 2 and 3
Q3. `for` loops are similar to `while` loops. How is a `for` loop different from a `while` loop?	`for` loops are used to loop a specified number of times
Q4. What would be a good time to use a `while` loop in a game?	to keep a game going while a certain condition is `True`
Q5. What symbol is used to write comments in the code that are not a part of the code?	#

Chapter 6, Working with Data – Lists and Dictionaries

Questions	Answers
Q1. What is the proper syntax to use when creating a dictionary?	{ }
Q2. What kinds of data can be included in one list?	All datatypes can be included a list
Q3. What is the proper syntax to use when creating a list?	[ ]

Chapter 7, What's in Your Backpack?

Questions	Answers
Q1. What is nesting?	When one item is inside of another item
Q2. What does the list called `players` organize in this game?	It organizes all items belonging to each player
Q3. What kind of item is inside of the `players` list?	A dictionary
Q4. What is a game loop?	2 and 3

Chapter 8, pygame

Questions	Answers
Q1. How do you start pygame?	`pygame.init()`
Q2. How do objects move in pygame?	Objects only appear to move, but they are actually constantly redrawn
Q3. How is an object redrawn using pygame?	`pygame.display.update()`
Q4. What is the shorthand used to identify keys in pygame?	pygame.K_keyname

Index

Made in the USA
Middletown, DE
09 April 2018